Coaching the Coach

Life Coaching Stories and Tips for Transforming Lives

Compiled by
Georgia Shaffer

Bold Vision Books
PO Box 2011
Friendswood, Texas 77549

©Copyright Georgia Shaffer 2013

Library of Congress Control Number: 2013935338
ISBN 978-0-9853563-2-3

Printed in the U.S.A.

Published in association with Books and Such Literary Agency.

Cover design by John Magee, www.johnmageedesign.com

BVB - Bold Vision Books
PO Box 2011
Friendswood, Texas 77549

Coaching the Coach

Other books by Georgia Shaffer

Taking Out Your Emotional Trash

How NOT to Date a Loser

A Gift of Mourning Glories

Coming in 2014

Avoiding the 12 Relationship Mistakes Women Make

Table of Contents

Introduction

As a beginning coach, I made plenty of mistakes and formed more than one bad habit. Thankfully, a wise coach advised me to continually update my knowledge and skills and to learn from the expertise of others.

Just as first-year teachers don't supervise student teachers, or inexperienced therapists don't oversee counselors who just graduated from college, it's crucial that we as coaches are open to learning from those more experienced in the coaching field. In *Coaching the Coach,* forty-nine coaches generously share their wisdom on topics from organizing the office to successfully ending a coaching relationship.

If you are just starting to coach or considering becoming a coach, you'll want to start with the first chapter of the book which focuses on beginning your coaching journey. You'll find the topics addressed, along with the names of the contributing coaches, in the table of contents.

If you're an experienced coach, however, you might choose to begin with a chapter covering an area in which you especially want to grow. For example, if you are feeling insecure about your ability to coach, be sure to read chapter three on facing your insecurities. If you're struggling with marketing or growing your business, then you'll want to read chapter four or thirteen. While the stories included are based on actual experiences, many of the names and identifying details have been changed to protect the clients' identities.

You need education and training to become a coach, but don't stop there. Continue to grow professionally by learning from the expertise of these and other competent coaches so you can be the best coach God created you to be.

To view additional coaching tips from some of the coaches featured in this book, go to www.CoachingtheChristianCoach.com.

10

Chapter 1

Beginning Your Coaching Journey

We can feel both empowered and humbled when we hear God's call to become a Christian coach. Our gifts, talents, temperaments, and personal histories prepare us along with our education and training.

Although our journey will be distinct, it will also have similarities to the following coaches' stories. Whether you boldly or tentatively take your first steps forward, understand that every coach battles fear and has moments of misgivings. Successful coaches, however, all persevere.

No matter where you find yourself today, never lose sight of the fact that who you are when no one is looking matters. Your ability to influence others positively will depend on it.

Your Coaching Journey Begins Here
Dwight Bain

This is the very portrait of a vocation: a thing that calls or beckons,
that calls inexorably, yet you must strain your ears to catch the
voice that insists on being sought, yet refuses to be found.

C. S. Lewis

Where does your coaching journey begin? I believe it begins when God uses you to make a positive difference in shaping another person's life. It's about being used as a messenger to communicate God's voice to someone who is open to hearing about a greater purpose. Your journey as a coach is about sensing and knowing how to draw the unique potential out of another person, so he or she can move forward to experience God's greater plan for his or her life.

To avoid confusion about ethical practices, always remember that counseling is about helping people past their pain to find stability again. Coaching is about helping people realize their potential as a man or woman of strength. They are quite different disciplines, but I believe each still involves a divine calling from God.

C. S. Lewis described it this way: "This is the very portrait of a vocation: a thing that calls or beckons, that calls inexorably, yet you must strain your ears to catch the voice that insists on being sought, yet refuses to be found." Did you hear the part about quietly listening for the "still small voice" as Elijah called it (1 Kings 19:11-12 NKJV)? If you have a call on your life as a coach, then you need to listen quietly to what the Spirit is stirring up inside you. If it's God, then you won't be able to quiet that stirring until you move forward toward action. At least that's how my journey as a coach began.

God's Call on Me

More than thirty years ago I sensed God's call on my life to become a Christian counselor. My mentor, Elmer Towns, co-founder of Liberty University, describes the call of God on your life first as a "call to prepare," and prepare is what I did. In college and seminary, I was driven to learn everything possible about Christian counseling. I listened to Christian radio programs, read every book and magazine, and attended every workshop and seminar I could find, since there weren't many resources in the 1970s for this emerging professional industry.

It was like a dream come true in 1984 when a friend and I started a Christian counseling center in Orlando. We became the most trusted agency in our area by living out the call of God to help people in crisis find calm again. It was God's vision, lived out through the lives of two young seminary graduates who quietly listened for His voice.

Then more than twenty years ago that calling started to stir inside me again, in part due to the frustration I experienced over a dysfunctional counseling cycle that repeated too many times. Maybe you've seen it too. It went like this. Someone would call in a crisis, barely surviving. We would aggressively guide them through the stress to find stability and then send them home from counseling with high hopes for a better future. Unfortunately, two years later the person's life crashed again and we were back into Crisis Counseling 101, just to keep the person from drowning in problems. Something big was missing from the process, but what was it?

That's when I began to sense that same gentle voice asking questions like these: "What if there was a new way to help people? Would you be willing to learn the skills to guide people past their pain toward their potential?"

My answer was, "Absolutely!" It made perfect sense to learn how to better serve regular people who missed God's purpose not because they were stuck in misery, but because they were beyond misery; they were stuck in mediocre.

Then it got exciting. God's Spirit stirred up the desire to learn more about taking people to a new level of success, and the search began again. Professional coaching hadn't been invented yet, but a number of voices in the marketplace were coming together to discuss how to guide people toward their potential. Creative minds like Thomas Leonard, Patrick Williams, Dan Sullivan, Babs Smith, Chris McCluskey, John Nagy, Ken Blanchard, Laurie Beth Jones, John Maxwell, and countless others were thinking creatively about how to take average people and help them achieve above-average results. God began to allow me to connect with like-minded people who were sensing the same desire to make a positive difference.

My First Coaching Process

I believe coaching is a journey, one that flows out of your life story. That journey for me was through speaking to business groups. I first heard the term "life coach" after speaking to a Fortune 500 company in the early 1990s when a member of the audience asked if I offered executive coaching. I wasn't sure what that person was asking, so I took down the person's phone number and promised to call back. After doing some research about getting trained and certified in this new discipline, I called back and we began the coaching process. The stirring in my spirit was a reflection of another call to prepare—not just as a counselor, but also as a coach.

Maybe my story sounds a lot like your story. Maybe God is already stirring you to be part of something more, part of the next wave of helping people, and not just as a coach, but as a distinctively Christian coach. There is a difference.

Who knows? Maybe you will be a pioneer in the process of Christian coaching. Maybe your name will be among those listed as the early voices who said, "There needs to be something better for coaches, something clearly Christian—something like 'X.'" I hope so, and I hope to encourage you on your journey of being the messenger of God's voice to take average people past mediocrity to experience God's vision for their lives.

Coaching the Coach Tip

If you have been searching for the next chapter in your journey as a people helper, perhaps coaching is the answer. There is no better place to start than with the largest group of Christian coaches in the world, the International Christian Coaching Association (ICCA). If you are sensing God's call on your life to prepare to serve others as a coach, I invite you to visit ICCA's website at www.iccaonline.net, or you can also visit www.LightUniversity.com since there are almost 200 hours of online Christian coach training programs available. Both of these organizations are dedicated to equipping you to make a positive difference in our world for Jesus Christ.

Building Your Confidence as a Coach
Sandra Dopf Lee

Commit your work to the Lord, and then your plans will succeed.
Proverbs 16:3

Coaching is one of the fastest growing careers today as our society looks for guidance and new ways to navigate through challenges and excel. Although the coaching profession has grown exponentially over the last several years, it has experienced a few growing pains. There are still some professional disciplines that do not recognize coaching as the viable and influential career that it is today. This can be discouraging for some coaches—especially those who are just beginning their careers. I have identified three key reasons why coaches are sometimes misunderstood or misrepresented as they build their practices.

1. Some Coaches Lack Proper Education

Unfortunately, there are professionals who have not taken the time or opportunity to understand the field of coaching for what it is and what it is not. They represent themselves as coaches without the proper training and qualifications.

2. Coaching as a Professional Career is Still Relatively New

Potential clients do not know coaching is an option or understand the value of being coached.

3. Some Coaches Fear the Unknown

Will they find enough clients to support their business? Will they have the wisdom to know which professionals to partner with and which ones will cause more harm than good?

When I began my practice as a divorce coach, I faced every one of these issues. I obtained the necessary formal education and practical experience and did not associate with frauds. I came to realize, however, that the two biggest hurdles in my career were educating my clients and educating other professionals in the value of my services to divorcing couples.

Many people recognize and accept a life coach, a health coach, and a financial coach to name a few. This is partly because some famous television personalities have helped educate the public about the benefits of working with a coach. However, a divorce coach is still very new. A Christian divorce coach, like me, is even less understood and recognized.

I wrestled with God for several months believing that I must not be following His plan if I thought I was to become a divorce coach. How would other Christians perceive my career? Would they believe I was promoting divorce? Would they believe I was going to make it easier for couples to divorce? Would people question how I could call myself a Christian, yet choose this as my career path?

Once I surrendered and truly knew within my soul that I was being called to this new career as a divorce coach, then I faced an all-together different set of questions and doubts. Would I be able to earn an income as a Christian divorce coach? How would I educate my prospective clientele about this area? How would I ever find the confidence to work with attorneys?

I'd had limited experience working with attorneys: when I closed three home purchases, prepared my will, and got a divorce. My take-away from these five experiences was that all attorneys seem to speak a different language than I do; they all seem way smarter than I am; and they all seem to make a lot more money than I do. I knew I wouldn't have to work with attorneys on a daily or weekly basis, but I did know as a divorce coach I would need to interact with them from time to time. I feared attorneys would not accept me as a professional nor would they accept my career as a legitimate practice.

In the beginning of my new career, some attorneys did not believe in me or the field of coaching. Many days I felt discouraged and wanted to give up and quit. I allowed self-doubt, the opinions of others, and my fears to go before what I knew to be true in my heart: that my life experiences, my education, and my life calling from the Lord had brought me to the career of divorce coaching. Other people's opinions of me or my profession did not matter; I was following God's greater plan for my life, and I knew He wanted me to stay the course.

Divorce is one of the most challenging and life-altering experiences a person can face. The emotional, financial, spiritual, and physical damage can often leave divorced people immobilized with fear, doubt, shame, and guilt. They struggle to see God in the midst of their pain, and they question God and their faith and beliefs. Their energy is usually expended on trying to "win" the divorce battle, living in the crisis, fearing the unknown, and just plain struggling to survive.

Children are usually the biggest victims in the divorce process. They have lost their family as they knew it; they won't have open access to both Mom and Dad as they had before the divorce, and they often feel caught in the crossfire between two fighting parents.

The divorce process has struggles and fears all its own, which are exacerbated by the legal system and working with attorneys. In the midst of all this angst, however, is a good time for the divorce coach to show up. We can help with a plan, putting structure around the conflict like no other professional does during this time. Ultimately, the hope of a Christian divorce coach is to bring the Lord's peace, strength, and leading into the process. We hope that others will see the hand of God at work in what Satan intends for total loss.

Attorneys' attitudes toward divorce coaching as a career began to change when they saw that clients' lives were being changed by the coaching approach. They saw that I cared for the entire family's well-being and shifted clients' focus toward healing and growth and not destruction. Attorneys witnessed divorcing couples learning to separate their issues as a couple from the need to continue to work on building a way to co-parent together for the sake of their children. God doesn't desire divorce, but when it happens, a trained and equipped coach can help people grow through and beyond their divorce into the life He still has for them to live.

Today, I am thrilled to say that by staying true to what I knew the Lord wanted me to do, I have had the opportunity to help hundreds of divorcing couples as they rebuild their lives. I'm glad I tackled my fear of working alongside attorneys years ago. I now find they respect and understand coaching as a profession, and we actually enjoy working as a team. I believed in my important work, and although it was not always easy, I stayed true to God's plan.

Coaching the Coach Tip

You have to believe in the viability of your career before you can expect other professionals to believe in you. The following tips are important to keep in mind as you build a thriving coaching practice.

First, believe in and respect your career. Then you can begin to expect others to respect you and your career as a coach.

Represent yourself as a professional in every area of your practice: in your personal presentation, in your written representation (business cards, print material, etc.), and in your online presence (your website, social media portals, etc.).

Join networking groups of other like-minded professionals that work with the same demographics or clients as you do. (For example, as a divorce coach, network with family counselors and financial advisors.)

Educate yourself about your colleagues' careers and look for ways you can partner with or complement each other.

Always be ready with a brief (thirty seconds to two minutes) explanation of your services in the event you have the opportunity to educate a professional or the public about the field of coaching and the benefits it has to offer.

A Rookie Coach Takes a Risk
Diane Schroeder

Trust God from the bottom of your heart; don't try to figure out everything on your own. Listen for God's voice in everything you do, everywhere you go; he's the one who will keep you on track. Don't assume that you know it all.
Proverbs 3:5-7 THE MESSAGE

It all started when I least expected it—my coaching career, that is—with my post on Facebook: "Kicking off my psychology program today at Cornerstone University. Wish me luck!"

The live-chat window popped up with a note from Jennifer. "Good luck with that, Diane! And why'd you choose psychology?"

"Spent two years seeking direction from God about what to do after my kids are gone, and believe He's leading me into life coaching and counseling."

A minute later my chat window came back with this: "Wish I knew what I was supposed to be doing; any ideas on how to figure it out?"

Jennifer's question both surprised and pleased me. I was a total rookie and not looking to build a practice. I was in the process of completing my life coaching certification, halfway through night courses for a bachelor's degree in psychology with a plan to get a master's in counseling for my Licensed Professional Counselor (LPC). In addition to being a student, I was also a busy mom with teens as well as a wife to a husband who traveled routinely for business. Most of my days were filled with my homework, laundry, cooking, and chauffeuring teenagers. It took all I had to keep up with life, so working with clients or building a practice wasn't on my radar.

Before I responded to Jennifer, I remembered a conversation with one of my mentors. "You know, Diane, you can start seeing clients as a life coach while you're going to school."

"Really? I can do that?"

"Sure. You start by charging a small fee, and as your experience and credentials increase, so will your fees. Once people start to see how much you can help them, they'll tell other people, and your client list will grow. By the time you graduate you'll have a practice."

Jennifer's question made me face the challenge (and fear) of stating what I had to offer her and of asking to be paid for it. My fingers tapped away: "Funny you should ask, because I'm starting to work as a life coach and only charge a pittance. I'd be happy to set up a time to meet and talk about some ways I could help you." Before I clicked the enter key, I muttered, "Okay, Lord, here goes. I'm going to put myself out there and trust You." Click.

I felt amazed with Jennifer's response. "Sounds great! I can only afford a pittance, so that's perfect. When can we meet?"

I was blown away. I thought for sure she'd say, "No, thank you." Instead, she became my first official paying client. We arranged to meet later that day. On the drive over, I prayed, asking God to show me how to handle the situation. It was an amazing, exhilarating, Spirit-led experience.

As I worked with Jennifer, God—like manna from heaven—continued to put people and situations in my way to confirm my career path in coaching. One such instance I like to call my "grocery store run-in."

Breezing through the soda aisle one afternoon, I passed a young lady who was chatting up a storm on her iPhone. She hung up, looked me square in the eye, and said, "I just got off the phone with a friend who told me she's looking for a marketing assistant and I'm really interested in it. I wonder what I should tell her."

Without skipping a beat, this stranger went on. "She's kind of a friend, and wouldn't it be weird if I told her I'm interested? And what if she turns me down? Wouldn't that make our friendship awkward? Should I just send her a text and see what she says?"

My gut reaction was to burst out laughing and ask about the hidden cameras, but I had enough sense to say, "How about I answer your questions with a question? Why are you asking me all this?"

"I don't know what to do, and you look like someone who would give me really good feedback."

I was stunned. I also saw the vulnerability it took for her to approach me, so I gave her the best response I could. "When opportunity knocks, definitely pursue it, especially in this economy. The worst that can happen is if she says, 'No.' But you'll never know unless you try. Don't text her either. Just give her a call and offer to buy her coffee, so you can discuss it face to face."

"Well, what if she says, 'No'? Won't it be weird if we have this awkward thing between us?"

"No, I don't think it'd be weird," I said. "Just respect her answer as the boundary she needs between work and friends and go on being friends."

"Oh, okay…I think I will. I feel so much better. Thank you!"

We hugged and exchanged business cards right in the middle of the soda isle, which was something I've never pictured myself doing. Who knows, perhaps someday my unexpected "grocery store run-in" will give me a call or pass my card along to someone else who needs coaching. Either way, I was delighted I could help her. When I think back about this experience, I view it as confirmation from God and a test of my willingness to make myself available when asked.

Coaching the Coach Tip

As a rookie coach I've experienced doubt and fear, such as wondering if I would be able to help others while still in training. I believe I am probably not alone in this, and other coaches may have had similar feelings. As I've begun my coaching career, I've had to depend on God to show me if and when I'm ready, and I have relied on trusted mentors to advise me. To succeed, I believe coaches need both a firm faith in God and accountability from experienced coaches.

A bad economy has also fueled other fears, as I've wondered whether I should get into the coaching business. To counteract these fears, I've developed a purpose/mission statement for my schooling and I am working on one for my business. When I have qualms about my career, my purpose statements are lodged in my brain as reminders of why I coach. The purpose statements help me a great deal, and I firmly believe coaches should develop a purpose statement to keep on track during times of uncertainty.

I also think it is critical for coaches to be in constant communication with God about who He wants them to help and why. I fondly recall the instances when God intervened, like with my first client Jennifer and my grocery store run-in, as concrete answers to prayer.

I also recommend that coaches use inspiring quotes to stay focused, like this one from Helen Keller, who said, "It is for us to pray not for tasks equal to our powers, but for powers equal to our tasks, to go forward with a great desire forever beating at the door of our hearts as we travel toward our goal."

God's Wake-up Call
Vicki Corrington

I have come that they may have life, and have it to the full.
John 10:10b

The glory of God is man fully alive.
St. Irenaeus of Lyon

Ten years ago, God set His alarm clock and woke me up to the reality that I'd lived on autopilot for so long it seemed there was nothing left of me. I had forgotten who I was. I had settled for doing what seemed right rather than being who He created me to be. I felt as if every mind-numbing insurance form and patient account detail that crossed my desk in my husband's chiropractic practice sucked a little more life out of me. That emptiness was the price of sleepwalking through life.

What did Jesus use to open my eyes and bring me back to the land of the living? The bottom line was the power of Christ-centered coaching combined with praying the Word.

That morning as I watched the fog lift over the mountains from the deck of our log home, my thoughts also cleared. God then gave me a mental checklist that would work for me:

- Hire an experienced coach. Check.
- Rediscover how God has wired me and choose to be fully me, fully alive. Check.
- Take personal responsibility for operating within my temperament, strengths, and gifting as much as it is up to me. Check.
- Set powerful goals that are within my ability and right to control. Check.

- Take action steps that line up with who I am and what is important to me. Check.
- Fully participate in professional Christian coach training to hone my own coaching skills. Check.
- Immerse myself in a community of coaches who affirm and value me and what I am called to do. Check.
- Be conscious of and honor how others are wired. Check.
- Talk their language. Check.
- Pass it on so others can take it and run with it. Check.

I began with the first item on my check list and hired professional coach Christopher McCluskey. My approach to the "Vicki Packet" he requested before our first session was eye-opening in itself. I prepared a three-ring binder full of both formal and informal assessments of my strengths and weaknesses, letters of recommendation from successful jobs as well as a job lost, creative project photos, and transcripts.

My ears perked up at my coach's words: "Wow, this really is a re-discovery process for you!" Over time, his powerful questions drew out the purpose of my heart, which lined up with my own Myers-Briggs results: to make a difference in creative and insightful ways that help people grow.

Judy Santos, who launched the Christian Coaches Network in 1998, warned me one week, saying, "You can't hit a home run every time, Vicki!" and the next week, said, "You're the best I've ever seen at this temperament-based coaching." Her affirmation deepened my sense of calling to facilitate this process of cooperating with God's design for those who are ready and coachable.

My coaches' respectful, honest, and challenging feedback, as well as opportunities to step outside of my comfort zone to serve as a faculty member in the world of professional Christian coaching, came with the opportunity to say "Yes," "No," or "Renegotiate."

I am honored they saw the real me in spite of my struggles and welcomed me warmly into their community of coaching colleagues.

This dynamic process accomplished God's life-giving work in me. These days, "Fully You, Fully Alive" is more than my tag line; it is a recurring theme through my life coaching, mentor coaching, and retreat coaching, all of which are temperament-based.

What's my powerful goal? To be just plain Vicki with Christ as my life, to be the best Christian coach God will have me be, and as much as it depends on me, to help others live out their unique God-given purpose in a way that brings them life and Him glory.

God knew I needed an experienced, competent coach who cared enough to focus on my agenda; to be fully present in co-creating our relationship of trust and intimacy; to communicate effectively through deep listening, powerful questions, and direct communication; and to encourage my personal responsibility for doing the work that would give the greatest sense of progress between sessions.

These are the basic coaching competencies we need to practice and demonstrate with such a high standard of excellence that we are then freed up to bring our own essence and being into the conversation. I am confident that as we join in community with other experienced Christian coaches, our clients will be better served, our collective vision will be strengthened, and God will be glorified.

How I approach coaching is personalized to most effectively draw out clients of various personality styles, strengths, and preferences. Your insights into what motivates your client (what to say "Yes" to) as well as potential Achilles heels (what to self-manage) can be invaluable in your shaping powerful questions to help your clients achieve awareness in their lives and figure out how they can realize their dreams. I've learned that what I needed as a client plays an important role in what I am inspired to give my coaching clients and my students in the Essentials of Coaching classes, Coaching Skills Development practicum, and Coaching Skills Mastery practicum I teach.

My way of organizing my first packet stands out in sharp contrast to how some of my clients handle their initial packets. Scribbled notes and goals presented on a napkin immediately before a coaching session don't necessarily show lack of motivation but speak volumes about the need to take into account individualized approaches and styles.

For me, an extrovert, I enjoy the give and take of a coaching session with interactive conversation where we can brainstorm and launch new, challenging pursuits. I find this even more energizing than drinking a steaming hot cup of coffee.

I thank God for His gracious wake-up call. He took what I needed to learn, combined it with my strengths and preferences, and turned it into a blessing that goes beyond all I could ask or imagine in my second half of life.

Coaching the Coach Tip

In addition to opening my eyes so many years ago, God also opened my ears before I could open my mouth as a coach. So when meeting with clients, I keep in mind the acronym ACT, which will also help you as a coach:

- Be **A**ware of how you, the coach, are wired. What energizes you? How do you take in information? How do you prefer to make decisions? How do you like to approach your world?

- Be **C**onscious of how your clients are wired. What energizes them? How do they take in information? How do they prefer to make decisions? How do they like to approach their world?

- **T**alk your client's language. How can you communicate in ways that show you understand what's important to them? What will draw out the purposes of his or her heart? What word pictures would take the conversation to a deeper, more meaningful level?

27

When you begin to talk your client's language, you will discover new ways to coach in the two major areas that potentially drain people the most. The first area is unresolved conflict, and the second is operating outside of their strengths, temperament, and gifting. If you can help a client address these two areas, you energize each one to pursue true passions and bring added value to the coaching relationship. It pays to respond to God's wake-up call!

The Power of Influence
Dr. Tim Clinton, Ed.D.

A good name is more desirable than great riches;
to be esteemed is better than silver or gold.
Proverbs 22:1

L iars. Cheaters. Sex scandals. These days, a good name is hard to come by. Self-satisfaction and pleasure are "in," and in a lot of ways integrity and godliness are "out." Have you noticed that anyone with character is constantly being pounded and examined to find that flaw?

Battle through it all. Your influence as a Christian coach starts with your character—who you are in the dark. You can't separate your professional and personal lives because ultimately, your work as a coach flows from the person you are when no one is watching. When considering our personal character, we must examine four key areas: our identity, foundations, relationships, and motives.

Identity

What defines you as a person? Integrity, honesty, and determination? Or selfishness, laziness, and cutting corners? In a culture that glorifies sin, it's easy to make excuses. But we need look no further than the daily news to see the real truth—any sin we secretly harbor will eventually destroy us, our influence, our public voice...even the relationships we treasure the most.

Character, in my mind, is perhaps the most neglected area of development. You can have the best social media platform and blog design, but clients won't seek you out as a Christian coach if they don't believe you, feel safe with you, trust you, admire you, and want to learn from you. You can get the top coaching training in the world, but if you're not a man or woman who is true to your word, your influence will be short-lived.

Character is anchored by wisdom. That's why Solomon wrote, "Wisdom is the principal thing; therefore get wisdom. And in all your getting, get understanding." The Greek word for "principal" here is rê 'šît, which literally means "the first thing; the very beginning." Seeking God's wisdom through His Word, prayer, and godly counsel must be your first priority in your coaching business.

Foundations

What are you building your business on? As a Christian coach, your work should be distinctly Christian. Developing godly character—ultimately becoming like Jesus—must be at your core. "Let each one take care how he builds…For no one can lay a foundation other than that which is laid, which is Jesus Christ," Paul challenges us. "Now if anyone builds on the foundation with gold, silver, precious stones, wood, hay, straw—each one's work will become manifest, for the Day will disclose it, because it will be revealed by fire, and the fire will test what sort of work each one has done."[2] You can't give well what you don't do well.

Relationships

You are who you spend time with. Who is pouring into your life? As you empower and encourage others through coaching, you need people who are pouring into you. Isolate yourself and burnout is inevitable. As Christian coaches, we desperately need the truth of God's Word flowing into our lives. One of God's favorite ways to strengthen and establish us is through mentors, accountability, and godly friendships. Every Timothy needs a Paul, and every Paul needs a Timothy.

Being completely honest about our failures, sins, and weaknesses can be difficult, but it's the first step toward healing and growth. You're not that good. The sooner you learn this truth and seek out friends and coaches who speak truth into your life, the better! Otherwise, sin wreaks havoc in our lives and eventually will impact our business and destroy our good name. That's why God's

Word commands us, "Confess your sins to each other and pray for each other so that you may be healed."[1]

Scripture also tells us, "Plans fail for lack of counsel, but with many advisers they succeed."[2] Even as you're working on your business plan, make sure to seek out godly advice from people who you trust.

Motives

Why do you want to be a Christian coach? This may seem intuitive, but stop and think. Wanting to help and empower others is a noble calling, but what's beneath that? Are you driven by the praise and approval of other people—seeking to build your "public image"? Maybe you mistakenly feel pressure to rescue other people and become "God" in their life. The reality is that people don't care how much you know until they know how much you care.

J. B. Miller put it well when he wrote, "No one can understand that mysterious thing we call 'influence'…yet every one of us continually exerts influence—either to heal, to bless, to leave marks of beauty, or to wound, to hurt, to poison, to stain other lives."[3]

Ultimately, for lasting change and growth to happen in a client's life, the Holy Spirit must move through you. So seek God first. Listen for His voice. And guard your heart against the arrogance that success often breeds. "Humble yourself in the sight of the Lord and he will lift you up."[4] Love God and love others…in that order.

"A good name is more desirable than great riches." What do people think of when they hear your name?[5]

---

1 Proverbs 4:7, NKJV

2 1 Corinthians 3:10-13, ESV

1 James 5:16, NIV

2 Proverbs 15:22, NIV

3 J. R. Miller, "The Influence of Companionship," Retrieved December 6, 2012 from http://gracegems.org/Miller/influence_of_companionship.htm

4 James 4:10, NIV

5 Re-printed from *Christian Coaching Today* Volume 2, Issue 2 with permission of the International Christian Coaching Association/American Association of Christian Counselors.

Chapter 2

Launching Your Coaching Business

Launching a coaching practice can be intimidating for even the most confident entrepreneur. How do you move from thinking or talking about being a coach to actually stepping out to become one?

A good way to start is to remember who God is rather than becoming paralyzed by your own insecurities. Talking to and listening for God's guidance about the vision and direction of your practice is essential, as is praying for and with your clients. As you begin your coaching practice, think carefully about your identity as a Christian. Unfortunately, the world seems to hold Christians to a higher standard. The bad practices of one Christian coach can radiate negative light onto other Christian coaches.

Having your own coach is helpful, too. He or she can guide you in compiling and creating the forms and procedures best suited for your coaching practice. Paying a bit of attention to the details now will save you time in the long run.

Steps to Launching a Successful Business
Georgia Shaffer

Don't be afraid, because the Lord your God will be
with you everywhere you go.
Joshua 1:9b NCV

A lack of confidence often paralyzes coaches who are just launching their businesses. One coach emailed me, saying, "I am stressed over the idea that people are now going to be paying me. Will I give them enough value for their money?"

Another coach who was about to start his business said, "I'm worried about letting my clients down."

When thoughts like these start to haunt you, remember you are not alone. Moses was called by God, but he immediately responded, "Who am I?"

If Moses was called today to be a coach, he might ask, "Who am I to even think I can be a coach? Who am I to think I'm ready to launch a coaching business and be paid for my services?"

It doesn't matter who you are. What does matter is who God is. Just as He was with Moses, God will be with you. Therefore, the first step in launching your coaching business is to reflect on God and His attributes.

Reflect on Who God Is

Immerse yourself in Scripture that reminds you of the presence and power of God. For example, read the stories of Moses and Joshua and remember that just as God equipped these two men, He can equip you.

As you reflect on the attributes of God, take an honest assessment of yourself. Do you believe God is creative and powerful enough to make a coach out of you? Do you believe He has the ability to do this even if you feel as though you're not gifted in coaching? What do you believe about God's ability to develop your talents and to use you in the lives of others?

When you recognize your humble dependence on God and His power to enable you to achieve His purposes, that's when He can use you to transform the lives of those you coach.

Get a Coach

Many who are first starting their businesses find it helpful to have a coach for support and guidance. Remember, Moses didn't go it alone either. He had his brother, Aaron, for support, and he took wise advice from his father-in-law, Jethro (Exodus 18).

I often find that the clients I coach need a combination of encouragement and a gentle push. One beginning coach emailed me several times the day before her first appointment with a paying client. She was terrified. With some support and genuine encouragement on my part, however, she was able to push past her fears, lean on God, and take the risk. She kept reminding herself that God is powerful enough to coach her and sure enough, her first session as a coach went extremely well.

Experienced coaches can also help you by sharing valuable information they learned from other coaches along the way. For example, one of my coaching friends shared that she learned from her coach how offering packages, a three- or six-month coaching program, was very successful. When I passed this idea on to another coach, she had such great results that she said, "Make sure you include this marketing strategy in your book *Coaching the Coach*."

You might offer, for instance, a six-month plan that gives the client at least a 15 percent savings compared to the price they would pay for individual sessions. Or maybe you create the option that if they sign up for a twelve-month plan, they save 20 percent over the per-session fee. If you want to see a listing of different services and payment plans, you can find the specific coaching programs I offer for coaches, communicators, and women on my coaching page at www.GeorgiaShaffer.com.

Organize the Details

Beginning coaches also need to organize their offices and attend to the administrative details. Decide on the key coaching questionnaires and inventories you like to use, and then personalize them with your business name or logo. If an inventory or assessment is copyrighted, you definitely need to keep the copyright information on the document and give credit to the original author. Where possible, you want a standard look for the documents you use with your clients.

For example, in the top left corner of my welcome letter, client data form, and pre-session questionnaire I have my logo with the stylized words "what needs to Grow, what needs to Go." (You can see some examples of how I personalize my documents by visiting my free resources page at www.GeorgiaShaffer.com.) As one coach said, "Giving my inventories or articles a professional look builds my confidence and reminds me of the fact that I am a professional coach."

I then store all these templates in one file folder named "Coaching Tools" under "My Documents" on my computer.

Decide also how you will keep track of your clients' emails, their completed inventories, and their pre-session forms. For each client, I have a physical file folder, labeled with his or her name, stored in a file cabinet. I usually keep a copy of the life-coaching agreement and other key information, such as the client data form, in that file. You, however, might not have space for file cabinets or they might be filled with other documents and information. One of the coaches I worked with has her assistant electronically scan the various inventories and assessments and store them on her computer.

For emails, I copy or drag all correspondence into separate Outlook folders labeled with the client's name. I also keep another electronic folder with each client's name in a folder labeled "Coaching" under "My Documents." And I regularly back up my computer files on an external hard drive.

Because we are all subject to the possibility of a computer crash, fire, robbery, or computer virus, we are wise if we back up our computer files offsite. Whether you use iCloud or pay for a service like Carbonite, decide how you will back up your clients' key information. For example, one of my friends had her laptop stolen, and the offsite service enabled her to retrieve all her files.

Finally, remember for tax purposes you need to report the income you receive from each client. It's best to consult your accountant to find out what format he or she prefers you to use, such as QuickBooks or Excel.

In addition to keeping records, part of organizing your business details may also include offering services such as voice and video sessions over the Internet (also known as Variable I/O Port, or VIOP). Skype and Tango are common VIOPs that coaches use to connect with their clients. Some clients find that the cost of their time or money to learn how to use these services outweighs any benefits, while others enjoy using them and want to see their coach's face during sessions.

Another service I provide for my clients, at no extra cost, is the option of recording their coaching sessions. This gives them the opportunity to go back and listen to their conversations with me. I've successfully used Freeconferencepro.com. If you use this option, you need to set up an account before you begin working with a client. Once you have an account, you will need to schedule each session on the website and send your client a phone number and an access code. After each coaching session, you can download the MP3 file and email it to the client as an attachment. One thing you need to make clear up front is that if your client has limited long distance or pays for telephone service by the minute, in contrast to unlimited long distance, the client will have to pay for the phone call.

The advantage of attending to these details ahead of time is that later you are able to focus more on meeting the needs of your clients. The beginning stages of launching a coaching business can seem daunting, but the rewards of helping people change their lives are great. To move forward you need only take one step at a time. The first step is to reflect on God and His attributes. Then, find a coach and get busy organizing your details. With God's power working in and through you, you will help others grow.

Coaching the Coach Tip

Throughout your coaching career, pause often and reflect on who God is. Find verses in Scripture that encourage you and help you focus on God. One of my favorite verses reminds me I'm not alone: "I will instruct you and teach you in the way you should go; I will counsel you and watch over you" (Psalm 32:8).

Reading this book and referring back to portions of it as necessary is a good way to be coached, but also consider enlisting the aid of a professional coach.

If you dislike dealing with details, you may be tempted to overlook or avoid getting your office documents organized. Resist that temptation, because attending to these business tasks is what helps you become a professional coach.

Listening to God about Your Practice
Matthew Reed

For I know the plans I have for you, declares the Lord, plans
for welfare and not for evil, to give you a future and a hope.
Jeremiah 29:11 ESV

I entered the world of coaching for one primary reason: I had a great coach. I was blessed to spend the better part of a year working with Fran LaMattina, MCC. Fran helped me navigate a season in which I left my role as staff pastor at one of America's 100 fastest-growing churches. I spent a great deal of time in prayer and searched for God's next steps for me, and He clearly led me to coaching.

During my training as a coach at the Professional Christian Coaching Institute, I participated in a thorough discussion of the power of a compelling life vision, purpose, and mission. I felt like my long season as a pastor and my gifting as an encourager made coaching the clear path for my life, but having a life vision to be a great coach wasn't compelling for me. I needed a different vision. I also learned in my training that the one important dynamic that gives us as Christ-centered coaches a genuine leg up on others in our field is that we aren't alone in our process. We have the power of God aligning us, guiding us all along the journey of coaching. We see how God intervenes all the time with clients, but sometimes we forget that God is also present in the development of our practices.

I began to turn to God and ask Him to reveal a clear and compelling vision for my coaching practice and my life. I felt foolish that I hadn't really asked God what my version of coaching should look like and who I should coach. He provided amazing clarity and gave me a clear vision for practice: "Make the world a more effective and God-honoring place through coaching."

When I first put these words on paper, it felt far too audacious, too lofty. I nearly threw it away forever, but again God intervened and reminded me that since He provided the vision, He'd provide the method. But how could a coach, especially one with limited experience, "make the world a more effective and God-honoring place"? He was weaving that together, too.

During my last assignment as a pastor, I was responsible for reaching out into my community. As a part of that, I worked with the local chapter of the Christian Medical and Dental Association (CMDA). I was honored to serve as their chaplain. During that time, I recognized a repeated theme: Doctors have lives that are far out of balance. Scheduling time for them to fellowship together was almost impossible because of the frantic pace mandated by their careers. My anecdotal experience with the CMDA led me to explore the world of medicine and burnout. The results were alarming.

Medical professionals, doctors in particular, are exhausted and leaving the field unlike any other time in history. According to a University of Rochester School of Medicine study, more than half of all doctors are facing burn out. More than 30 percent of all doctors say that they would like to be out of medicine within the next five years. Looming medical reforms, greater legal risks, and convoluted spider webs of insurance reimbursement have doctors and other medical professionals looking for a way out. Having fewer doctors creates a greater societal need for those that exist. As a result, we have less availability to medical care. And even more stress is placed on the doctors who remain.

The general perception that doctors are unhappy means many highly capable students that would have entered medicine a generation ago are instead looking for other career paths. This results in fewer future medical advances. Society needs good doctors and medical professionals. The world can be more effective and God-honoring with more effective and God-honoring medical workers.

During my season of soul searching, the CMDA chapter invited Dr. David Levy to speak to local medical professionals. Dr. Levy is a world-renowned brain surgeon and the author of Gray Matter in which he details his spiritual transformation when he started praying with his patients. His presentation was amazing and informative. In the middle of it, Dr. Levy threw a curveball to the crowd by talking about the Sabbath—taking one day in seven to rest and worship.

"I take a twenty-four-hour period each week off, but it wasn't always that way," Dr. Levy said. "I was raised with an understanding of the Sabbath, but as I became a doctor I was taught that I was exempt from it. I took pride in that." Dr. Levy learned, though, that the concept of observing the Sabbath is good for everyone. "I have to fight for it and schedule it."

Dr. Levy talked about how important it is to totally unplug, which he inferred meant no phone, no media, and so forth. He talked about how the brain physically needs this rest to properly balance and how productivity increases when we unplug.

While listening to Dr. Levy, I received my final confirmation; God was going to use me to impact the world by coaching doctors and medical professionals.

Immediately after this evening with Dr. Levy, God started sending influential medical clients my way. The chief operations officer of one of America's largest healthcare networks asked me to be his coach. His goals were to improve the balance between his work and personal life and to establish his priorities. Another client was a health physicist at a globally renowned cancer treatment facility. He needed help at staying mentally and emotionally present at home with his family.

I've learned so much by working as a coach, particularly in the medical community. Medical professionals are deeply rewarding to coach because of their purposefulness to do the needed hard work. They see the value of ongoing professional development, so the act of personal development seems natural to them.

I've found that there are few coaches reaching out to medical professionals and virtually none from a Christ-centered perspective. I am grateful that God gave me a vision to make the world a more effective and God-honoring place through coaching.

Coaching the Coach Tip

It's easy as a Christian coach to see things like our niche or our marketing strategy as purely secular endeavors. In reality, God uses these things, like showing me the niche of coaching doctors, to reveal His larger will. We encourage our clients to listen to God through the process, and we try not to rush to develop a strategy. Often for our own practices, however, we put some things, like which niche to pursue, into the secular box and rush to strategize without first flooding our thoughts and ideas in prayer and listening to God.

God has plans for each of us. Talking and listening to Him is vital for discovering those plans. Without talking to God, and looking and listening for where He was speaking, I would have missed the best strategy for my coaching practice, God's.

Chapter 3

Facing Your Insecurities as a Coach

I haven't met a coach who doesn't question whether or not he or she is good enough to be a coach. Questions I most frequently hear are these: Am I good enough to be paid? Am I good enough to help my client get results? Am I good enough to maintain a successful coaching practice?

Insecurities are a normal part of being a coach, but that doesn't mean we should ignore them. The essays in this section will help you deal well with your insecurities. Beware of hiding in your baggage, as Saul did. Own your insecurities and fears, so you can disown them before they steal your confidence and your career. Most of all, keep your eyes on Christ, the author and perfecter of our faith—and your coaching business.

Confidence...After One More Class?
Renee Oscarson

In God I have put my trust, I shall not be afraid.
What can man do to me?
Psalm 56:11 NASB

Should I register for another class? I wondered. I had one course left to complete the requirements for the Accredited Coach Training Program. Because the Supervision Practicum course had been added after I began the program, I did not need to take that class. But I lacked confidence in my abilities as a coach. Taking an advanced class seemed like a good idea.

The course required that students have at least three coaching clients and be a Certified Life Coach or an Associate Certified Coach. I qualified.

As a university faculty member, I have the privilege of coaching graduate students through their final projects. Many students do not graduate because they leave school without completing thesis or dissertation requirements. Jan, one of the first students I coached (versus advised) through a thesis, told me, "I finally realized that this thesis wasn't going to write itself!" The structure provided by regular coaching sessions and coaching agreements enables students to take responsibility for their progress.

Because "life happens" during the process of completing a thesis, thesis coaching often includes some life coaching. Sue, one of my three clients at the time I registered for Supervision Practicum, wrote in an email that she would "choose [me as] an advisor because

[she] would get the benefit of a life-coaching paradigm." She added that she was "inspired by [me] academically." Likewise, I was inspired by her ability to think deeply about issues. We got along well, and I agreed to be her thesis coach.

I mentally reviewed the International Coach Federation (ICF) Code of Ethics. Sue was experiencing family challenges. She also had a conflict with another professor. I was concerned about her, but she assured me that she was seeing a counselor and she acknowledged that she understood the differences between coaching and counseling.

In our first interview, Sue described her potential thesis topic and shared her values, describing herself as "radical." I knew that in order for her to make an informed decision about working with me on a value-laden project, I would have to share my beliefs with her, since I describe myself as "moderate." Since she cancelled several coaching sessions, some time passed before I was able to bring up the topic of values. Good social science thesis research often involves both the advisor and advisee examining their own assumptions, and I looked forward to the challenge of coaching her through her project, even though neither of us was likely to change our beliefs.

The ICF Code of Ethics does not prohibit dual relationships, and clients are believed to be "creative, resourceful, and whole." I was Sue's instructor as well as her coach. This did not seem unusual to me because faculty members often have the dual roles of instructor and thesis advisor. Instead of advising, I was coaching. Yet I did have the responsibility (and power) of assigning a grade.

Our coaching relationship ended when final grades were posted. Although Sue passed the class, her grade was not as high as she would have liked; she believed that I had not given her life challenges enough consideration when assigning final grades. When she contacted me about her grade, she also informed me that the discussion about our value differences was not helpful. We talked once or twice after the course ended; however, she left school, and I had not seen her since the class ended.

One day I received an email and phone call from Sue that frightened me. She was considering taking action against me. I was afraid for my reputation and fearful of repercussions at work.

Discussions with a mentor reinforced that I had followed ICF ethical standards. I was participating in the Supervision Practicum course at the time the coaching relationship with Sue ended. When I began the course, I didn't understand how the course topics of transference and counter-transference related to coaching. Although the terms sound intimidating, transference occurs in most of our relationships because our past experiences impact how we relate to other people and situations. Transference takes place in coaching, however, when a client projects or redirects emotions stemming from past interactions to the coach or coaching relationship. Similarly, counter-transference takes place when a coach has an emotional response to the client or coach-client relationship, which is connected to earlier experiences.

During the course, I saw the concepts in action as accusations about unethical behavior tapped into my fears. My confidence was shaky to begin with, and working with Sue destroyed what little I had. I am thankful I had supportive colleagues in class and an experienced mentor during this time.

What might I have done differently? I have had good coaching relationships with other thesis students, as well as non-students, since this experience. I recently reviewed email exchanges I had with Sue in an attempt to understand the failed coaching relationship.

I identified several problem areas. In hindsight, and due to additional information, I could argue that Sue's run-in with another professor should have led me to be more cautious in partnering with her on a thesis. But if that were a criterion, some students would never get a coach, finish a thesis, and graduate. Transference and counter-transference may have contributed to both of our strong emotions.

As a thesis coach, I maintained more detailed records than I may have as an advisor. According to my records, we had only a few coaching sessions. The records of email exchanges, adherence to ICF ethical standards, and participation in Supervision Practicum were important in helping me assess and process this difficult experience.

The major problem in my approach was that I relied on professional records and ethical behavior for my well-being. I sought to increase my self-confidence by being prepared, by adhering to ethical standards, and by seeking input from more experienced coaches. I should have placed my confidence in God. Because my ultimate source of confidence was misplaced, I was frightened by what Sue might do to me. Now I am growing in confidence in the God of all grace.

Coaching the Coach Tip

My experience taught me at least four good things that every coach would do well to remember.

1. Put Your Trust in God

You may find yourself lacking confidence in your coaching. Trust God. Ask for His help, His strength, His guidance. Remember that He is your source of power and confidence.

In my situation, my fears pushed me into closer fellowship with God. When you experience fear, turn to God in prayer. Seek His counsel through His Word.

2. Remain in Close Fellowship with God

Don't wait until you are fearful. As your focus on Him increases, fears will decrease. Be aware of your own unresolved issues. Your fear may stem from the thought that what might happen will be similar to a difficult event you experienced before. Be confident of God's love for you, knowing that He is in control.

3. Recognize That Risks Do Exist

Jesus called us to be "wise as serpents and yet as harmless as doves" (Matthew 10:16 J.B. Phillips New Testament). Pray for wisdom, and pray regularly for your clients. Wisdom requires that we be professionally prepared. Seeking adequate training is good as long as that training isn't our ultimate source of confidence. Be familiar with ethical standards for coaches. As your coaching skills develop, be sure that you have a mentor coach or a group of coaches to help you examine your actions, hold you accountable, and help you process challenging situations.

4. Seek God for Your Peace

God desires us to love Him more than we love what He has called us to do. When we do that, His peace permeates us. May it be "well with your soul" as you seek and honor God through your coaching.

Impeded by Our Baggage
Rosemary Flaaten

Forgetting what is behind and straining toward what is
ahead, I press on toward the goal to win the prize for
which God has called me heavenward in Christ Jesus.
Philippians 3:13b-14

Baggage can refer to the suitcases we take on trains, planes, and automobiles, but it also is a quasi-psychological term that refers to the emotional things that encumber us. Our baggage restricts our freedom, development, or adaptability.

Imagine being at a track-and-field meet. Imagine a young runner who is not wearing the best cleats and aerodynamic clothing but is wearing snow boots and carrying a suitcase loaded with textbooks. Now imagine that person attempting to jump hurdles. Getting over each hurdle would be a major feat, given the baggage he or she is toting.

After we have worked with our clients to help them identify their goals and choose a path that will help them realize these aspirations, our role as a coach is to point out the hurdles and hindrances that pop up as our clients work toward these objectives. One of the benefits of having a coach is having an additional set of ears and eyes on the lookout for the baggage that weighs a person down.

But what about the coach? Do we as the coach have baggage that is holding us back?

A story in 1 Samuel 8-9 helped me see my baggage in a whole new light. Let me retell it: "We want a king!" demanded the Israelites. So God gave them the desires of their hearts and chose Saul whose view of himself was this: "I'm only a Benjamite, from the smallest of Israel's tribes and from the most insignificant in the tribe at that" (1 Samuel 9:21 NIV paraphrase).

One would think that Saul, having been chosen by the most highly respected prophet of the day, having been told that he was to become a leader for the people, and having experienced such personal transformation, would move into this new role with enthusiasm. Unfortunately, it didn't happen that way.

The people were assembled. The crown was ready. Saul's name had been called, but where was he? Samuel couldn't find him, so he inquired of God.

God's response should stop each one of us in our tracks. God found Saul, the man He had chosen and equipped to become king. Everyone discovered "he has hidden himself among the baggage" (1 Samuel 10:22b ESV). Saul's sense of inferiority based on his heritage became baggage that impeded his movement into the role God had for him.

This story resounds strongly with me. I grew up on a farm in a small, rural Canadian community with parents who lived simple lives. Emotional struggles were sidelined in favor of the philosophy of buck-up and work hard. Faith was uncomplicated and practical. Like Saul's view of self, "I'm only a Benjamite, from the smallest of Israel's tribes and from the most insignificant in the tribe at that," my view of myself was similar. "I'm only a little farm girl, from the smallest of families and from the most insignificant country at that." Thinking I was anything greater seemed pretentious and prideful.

Roll the clock forward thirty years: I have a master's degree in Christian counseling, I have successfully published two books, and I'm coaching individuals of substantial influence. But I still struggle not to hide out in the baggage of my heritage. My family origin of meager means becomes baggage that makes me hesitant to step into circles I would never have dreamed about as a child. My perception of my past keeps me from entering a client's world. I focus on the fear that I will have nothing of value to say to this influential person because of who I used to be. If I allow it, my baggage from the past pulls me away from relationships and creates obstacles hindering me from becoming who God has called me to be.

By studying Ephesians, I am learning how not to hide in my baggage. Paul, speaking about the mindset of non-believing Gentiles, describes baggage as "the futility of their thinking" (Ephesians 4:17). The word "futile" means that something is ineffective and useless. How have we come to think of ourselves as useless?

He also says, "they are darkened in their understanding" (Ephesians 4:18). Darkness causes us to be cautious, even paralyzed, holding us back in fear. This leads to hardening of our hearts (Ephesians 4:18). A path that is walked over time and again becomes packed and hardened. As disciples of Christ, we don't want to think like unbelievers. Yet, how often have we replayed the message of our heritage, creating a rigid view and a hardened heart?

But listen to the hope that God offers in Ezekiel 11:19. "I will give them an undivided heart and put a new spirit in them; I will remove from them their heart of stone and give them a heart of flesh." We don't have to have futile thinking. We don't have to have an understanding of ourselves that is darkened and impossible to decipher. We don't have to live with a hardened heart.

Ephesians 4:22-24 sets a new course of action. "You were taught, with regard to your former way of life, to put off your old self, which is being corrupted by its deceitful desires; to be made new in the attitude of your minds; and to put on the new self, created to be like God in true righteousness and holiness."

Let's all stop hiding in the baggage compartment where we feel safe. Let's forget what is behind—our baggage—and press on toward the goal God has marked out for us.

Coaching the Coach Tip

There are three steps to learning a new way to think about yourself: Put off the old, allow God to change your attitude, and embrace the new you. The first step is to "put off." Like old clothing stripped off our bodies, we can be free of our baggage. We don't have to walk around encumbered with a view of ourselves that represents yesterday. God is offering us a new set of clothing, not to put on over the top of our old, but after we take off the old.

Second, after the old is gone, we are to allow God to change the attitude of our minds. Emotional baggage is not something physical that we carry around but rather a mental entity. It is the baggage of yesterday that God desires to deal with so that we can move away from the old view of self that restrains us. God is offering to change the attitude of our minds.

Third, as the final step, we are to embrace the new us. We are to wear the "new self, created to be like God in true righteousness and holiness."

Time and again we have all seen the baggage from the past that encumbers our clients, but we too are at risk. Our ancestral heritage, upbringing, the things we did as a teenager, or what we came to believe about ourselves in any of the past decades of our lives can become an inhibitor of what we are called to do. It doesn't have to be that way. We owe it to ourselves and our clients to do the hard work of handling our own baggage. Allowing God access to our hearts will provide the Holy Spirit with the opportunity to reprogram the way we think about ourselves so that we more closely reflect God's view rather than the warped view we have held. What an incredible opportunity to become more than we had ever dreamed possible.

What's holding you back?

Who, Me?
Linda Gilden

I can do all things through Christ who strengthens me.
Philippians 4:13 NKJV

No one can make you feel inferior without your consent.
Eleanor Roosevelt, *This Is My Story*

We think you are the one to coach this author through her book." The publisher's call surprised me. I had coached a few of their authors before but never one like Lin with such an amazing story or such a large platform from which to share it.

"But I'm not sure I can do it," I said. Doubt and insecurity came at me from all directions.

"Would you just take a look at the project and talk to the author? I'm sure you will change your mind. It's really an exciting story."

Agreeing at least on the exciting part, I said that I would talk to the author.

After reading through all the notes and the publisher's specifications, I called Lin. Exchanging a few pleasantries, I got to the purpose of my call. I asked, "Do you really think I can help you? After all, you are a highly successful African-American lawyer who has been through things I never even heard of. On the other hand, I am a white Baptist southern belle who blushes just reading your notes. I think you probably need someone who understands your life a little better."

"I think you are the perfect person. You don't know anything about me, just like my readers. You can ask questions and make sure we get everything really clear."

"I hadn't thought about that."

As I prayed about whether or not this was the right job for me, I realized Lin was right. I was starting this coaching job totally in the dark. I would be able to clarify her words so that the reader who knew nothing about her could understand.

Many times during coaching I am less confident than I should be. My melancholy personality makes me wonder how I can teach anyone anything. I look around at others who know so much more than I do about seemingly everything.

But then God gently reminds me where I started. As a beginning writer, I knew very little about the publishing business. I thought I knew how to write, after all, most of the time I had received good grades in English class. But the more I learned the more there seemed to be to learn.

As I learned how to write with excellence because of my calling as a writer and as I learned how to navigate the publishing world, people who were just starting out began asking me to share what I knew. Before long the question became, "Would you be my coach?"

Following Paul's example with Timothy, I continued learning all I could from the experts while passing along what I was learning to those who needed to learn.

As I worked with Lin, I enjoyed getting to know her. The research I did to learn about her former life was interesting and fun. A part of her life dealt with the drug world—a world I had no knowledge of. So how did I educate myself? By hanging out on the street corner and in dark alleys? Of course not. I called a friend, the local sheriff, and offered to take him and his wife out to dinner if he would teach me everything he knew about crack cocaine and those who used it.

When we arrived at the restaurant, he had a ream of printed material on the subject and we had a lovely visit during dinner. I quickly learned if I don't know how to do something, there is someone out there who does. I also learned that people are taken aback when a sheltered southern belle asks for instructions on how to make a crack pipe.

Paul instructed Timothy in ministry, realizing that his experience was valuable to his young friend. Each one of us can be a Paul to someone in our lives, whether in a coaching situation or in friendship. God has gifted each of us with wisdom and experience that can benefit those who are coming along behind us.

But if we do not continue to be Timothys and learn from the Pauls in our lives, we will become stagnant and exhaust our effectiveness as coaches.

Lin's book became very successful. The night we finished the manuscript and said goodbye was a sweet parting. But I knew that we would be forever friends. This southern belle had learned many great lessons about a culture she knew nothing about. And Lin? She learned a great deal, especially that everyone in the world didn't understand her world and that God's love bridges any gaps.

The next day when I answered my doorbell, the florist handed me two dozen yellow roses. A kind gift? For sure. A meaningful gift? Yes. Yellow roses are the symbol of friendship—in this case a lasting one that sprung from a coach's reluctance to follow her calling.

Coaching the Coach Tip

Don't underestimate your abilities. When God calls you to be a coach, He equips you for the task. You must continue training to be the best you can be. As you do, you will be able to coach those who are behind you in their journeys. Everything you learn helps you grow and makes you a better coach.

Paul was our model coach. He showed us how to walk alongside those we coach, not only teaching them in the areas of our expertise but also guiding them to walk closer to God in the process.

Though my initial conversation with Lin made me feel inadequate, the end result was an affirmation of security in the calling God has given me. He doesn't call us to know everything when we are starting out; He just wants a willingness and desire to be equipped for the tasks He gives us.

Right-sizing Our Pint-size Moments
Cheryl Scanlan

He must increase, but I must decrease.
John 3:30 NASB

My journey with Tracy Stevens, my mentor coach, began in a fairly simple and straightforward way. I learned the skills of coaching from her and we would review coaching sessions that I recorded. I desired to excel to the highest caliber coach as quickly as possible. Periodically, we would talk about my rates, my practice, and various details related to the company, but I tended to gloss over those subjects. I enjoyed developing the professional skills much more than I did thinking about my company as a business.

For a couple of years Tracy championed me in a subtle but sincere way, saying "you are more than you realize you are." But I couldn't receive it. My husband was telling me the same thing, "Cheryl, you are good!" My clients were telling me the same thing, but something in me told me different. Somehow whatever that voice was saying was tied directly to how I was managing my coaching practice.

Finally, one day Tracy offered a simple direct communication: "You are treating your business like a hobby." I paused in our conversation to consider her words. I liked treating my business as a hobby. One of my desires was consistently to under-promise and over-deliver in relationships. Having been in business before, I understood the mindset of working with a company, the expectations that develop from customers, and the pressure to deliver that arises in turn. If I turned Way of Life Coaching, LLC into a full-fledged business, perceptions would change and expectations from clients would rise. I didn't want that pressure, and I didn't want my clients disappointed. Another tough mental hurdle was that I didn't like the idea of viewing my clients as business transactions. These were people, and I truly was endeared to my clients. They were also my brothers and sisters in Christ. I wanted to treat them well.

Of course, each of these thoughts could readily be flipped onto their backsides like little bugs, ridiculously defenseless:

- "You set the expectation with your clients in your preliminary consultation. What expectations do you want to set?"
- "You want to treat your clients well. How reciprocal would you like that? If clients do not want to treat you well, then how long would you want to keep them as clients?"

So after exhaling all my diatribes and expounding on my lengthy discourses, Tracy brought me squarely back to the number-one concern that I had never articulated to her before.

Because of the trust we had by now built in our relationship, I was able to be brutally honest. "I'm feeling small," I said. "And when I feel small, I become immobilized."

There was a long pause.

I wondered how she was going to help me work through this one.

Recognizing all that was implied in my admission, Tracy said, "You are the same size; the arena is just getting bigger."

The word "arena" prompted a picture. A baseball field came into my mind. "I'm not ready to go into the major leagues," I said. "I like playing Little League. I'm comfortable where I am."

But as we talked further, I realized something. The ball field is exactly the same size whether I'm playing in the minors or the majors. The only difference is the size of the audience.

This awareness for most might be a "duh," but for me, it was an "aha!" I like to work behind the scenes, to develop others and then get out of the way and watch them flourish.

For instance, at one point, I was responsible for a parachurch care ministry. The leadership team was large, representing five different ministries. At an elaborate recognition dinner I had planned for the teams and their spouses, the senior pastor made a point of saying he needed to recognize me in front of the group. I was very uncomfortable with the idea, but he logically explained, "How can you recognize others if you yourself are not willing to be recognized?" And so, onto the stage I went. Working with each individual team was not so overwhelming, but standing before all of them was unnerving. The difference? The size of the audience.

Metaphorically speaking, I'd stepped out from the batter's box. My chest tightened as I looked up at the stands. So many people. But then I thought of the words in Hebrews 12:1-2. As runners, we need to run "the race marked out for us, fixing our eyes on Jesus." Runners coming toward home plate only have a chance when they focus on a few square inches of the base. Batters don't hit a home run by looking at the size of the crowd. They hit one out of the park by focusing on the ball.

Lord, redirect my eyes, I prayed. And suddenly, I found clarity and refocused on what I'd discussed with Tracy. I focused on being the best coach I could be for those I worked with, and honoring God and dignifying my clients through the process. The stands, the noise, the pressure to perform, the concern about how others might react if I didn't hit one out of the park was all behind me. The only thing that was before me was my desire to excel still more in Christ. I focused on the ball.

Now what to do with my business? As I make the main thing the main thing, many components of running a successful business that I previously avoided are now falling into place more naturally and comfortably:

- Quoting my rates? No hesitation.

- Setting a schedule that is supportive of my family and outside interests? Much less likely to compromise.

- Stepping into larger, professional coaching agreements? Eager to engage in the partnerships.

- Establishing new clients? Clear on those my company is to work with.

- Hiring support staff? Thrilled that my company is solid enough financially to contribute to other wonderful families.

- New opportunities coming along? Assess them based on the strategic goals of the business, not based on my insecurities.

Much of what I avoided I can now embrace with new tools and a new mindset. I still allow myself times to feel small but for a very different reason. I'm learning that a sense of vulnerability is not a bad thing. When I'm in a pint-size moment, it allows me to right-size my God again.

Coaching the Coach Tip

When I recognize that sense of feeling small creeping in, I give it permission to stay long enough for me to go to the Lord for three things:

1. Confession

I pray something like this: "Lord, I'm feeling timid and vulnerable. I do not want to act presumptuously against You, nor do I want to remain at a standstill where You are asking me to move. Help me to find You in the midst of this situation."

2. Assessment

I ask God, "Lord, what would You have me do with the information You have given me?"

3. Realignment

I verbally realign myself and God. "Lord, it is You who works in me to will and to work for Your good pleasure. You have equipped me for every good work that You have called me to do. Show me how I am to be about Your business in this business."

Then, I've found these questions to be helpful: Where do I need to adjust? Where do I need to pause? Where do I need to move forward?

Chapter 4

Marketing Your Coaching

New or frustrated coaches often ask, "Where do I find more coaching clients?"

Sooner or later they come to realize that marketing is an essential part of building a coaching business. They also discover it is a great opportunity to lean on God to show them the way.

If "marketing" is a word that paralyzes you, then think of it as an intentional way of making connections and building relationships. Instead of procrastinating, begin to develop the skills outlined in this chapter as you learn to communicate your distinctiveness and personality to potential clients.

Marketing: A Path to Trusting God
Kim Avery

Now faith is confidence in what we hope for and
assurance about what we do not see.
Hebrews 11:1

Before I entered the wonderful world of coaching, I was a practicing Licensed Mental Health Counselor. It was a fun and rewarding career and in some ways it was very simple. As a counselor, I was expected to counsel. They didn't hire me to balance the books, file for taxes, create websites, or send out newsletters. I counseled.

I awoke every morning, drove to the office, grabbed a stack of files from the secretary, walked into the waiting room, and called the first person's name. I didn't know how the person got to the waiting room or how he or she found our practice. Every morning they just magically appeared.

What escaped me in all my education and preparation for life coaching was the fact that the day I became a life coach, I also became an accountant, tax preparer, web designer, newsletter writer, and most importantly, a marketer.

I began marketing my coaching, as I suppose many people do, by staying firmly inside my comfort zone. After all, God had called me to become a life coach, so surely He would provide the clients. I talked to a few friends, mentioned my new service at my church and built an amazing website.

But the clients didn't come.

Clearly, God wanted me to grow in some new ways. God, I prayed, if you just show me what to do to get clients, I'll do it.

The next day my son pointed out a story in our local newspaper about a new networking group beginning in a nearby town. I had never been to a networking event where people from various lines of work meet and greet, but I felt this was God's path for me.

Fighting my nervousness, I gathered up my business cards and off I went. It's probably a good thing that I had no idea at the time just how much God intended to stretch me.

Dressed in my best business clothes, I arrived at the meeting determined to mix, mingle, and network with the best of them. I had a nice chat with the chapter president and had a long, meaningful conversation with a local entrepreneur. As far as I could tell, neither of them were necessarily potential clients, but at least those two people now knew my name.

The buffet line opened and all thoughts of further networking vanished in the ensuing stampede. I got my plate, piled it high with rice and rubber chicken, and managed to grab the last seat at the back of the room.

The gavel sounded and the meeting began. Shirley, the president, straightened her shoulders, gave a brief nod to our honored guest, and began to read an impressive list of our speaker's educational achievements and various accomplishments. She closed her introduction with a detailed summary of the speaker's business and carefully provided her contact information.

Amazing! Five minutes into the meeting, before the speaker even opened her mouth, this audience knew more about the speaker and her business than my best friend of twenty years knew about me.

All eyes turned to the speaker. She stood, moved to the front of the room, and wisely shared with us mere mortals the secrets of her success. We sat riveted. Obviously, we should listen. She stood at the front of the room, she wore the power suit, she was held in high esteem by our local president, and she was the expert.

It hit me. My all-out networking effort had netted me two iffy potential clients. In that same length of time, the speaker had fifty women who knew her, had grown to like her, and wanted to stay in touch with her.

Public speaking could be the answer to all my marketing woes. Of course, I had never given a speech before, and I had no idea how to do so. But in my heart, I knew God was asking me to step out in faith.

The meeting ended. With incredible fear and trepidation, I approached the chapter president. "Shirley, it occurred to me that as a professional life coach I have some great information that this group would really benefit from." Gulp. "I have a talk called 'From Ordinary to Extraordinary,' (well, I kind of, sort of thought about the topic a long time ago) and I would love (yeah, right) to present it at one of our meetings. Do you have an open slot that I could fill?" (Please say, "No." Please say, "No.")

"Yes," she exclaimed. "I'm sure they would love that. How about August?"

Before I knew it, I was committed. A myriad of thoughts flooded my mind as I drove home that day. I'm insane; what have I done? What if I bore them to death and the coroner has to come? What if I heard God wrong and this isn't of Him? Later I thought, if this doesn't work, next time I will schedule that delightful root canal instead.

I shouldn't have stressed. The speech was a success, and from that day on, my client schedule slowly began to fill. Each time I spoke publicly, I got at least one new client from the event.

Many years have passed since that fateful day at my first networking group, and God indeed works in mysterious ways. I've discovered that I love marketing, so much so that weekly I now have the privilege of coaching other Christian coaches and helping them fill their practices with eager clients.

But more than growing my own coaching business or helping other coaches do the same, I'm thankful to have learned firsthand that the God who calls us will also show us the way.

Coaching the Coach Tip

Marketing is more than just a necessary evil to be endured as we try to get clients. It is a critical part of our journey, designed to draw us closer to God.

It's natural to want shortcuts through the difficulties of building a coaching business. Like all of life, however, God has left challenges in our path so that in our areas of greatest weakness His strength will shine brilliantly.

For many, the idea of marketing fills them with fear and dread. For me, it was a path that brought me closer to God. What would change for you if you embraced marketing as part of your spiritual journey?

Networking
Rosemary Flaaten

*The successful networkers I know, the ones receiving tons
of referrals and feeling truly happy about themselves,
continually put the other person's need ahead of their own.*[1]
Bob Burg

*You're blessed when you're content with just who you are
—no more, no less. That's the moment you find yourselves
proud owners of everything that can't be bought.*
Matthew 5:5 THE MESSAGE

I walked into the elaborately decorated room certain that the only person I would know was the client who had invited me. This event had been billed as an excellent networking opportunity, so I eagerly accepted her invitation. I have never been one to shy away from situations where I do not know other people but have relished the opportunity to expand my circle of acquaintances. Who knows, maybe I'll even meet my next best friend.

As I mingled alongside my client, I quickly observed how well-connected she was within this group of exceptional women in powerful positions. I shrugged off the little voice in my head that screamed that I didn't fit into this crowd and instead set out to meet as many people as I could that evening. My goal was not simply to be introduced to one woman after another but to be as friendly as possible and to have some meaningful conversations. From experience I have learned that if I am genuinely interested in and curious about the person to whom I am talking, networking occurs. Conversely, if my goal is simply to promote myself and get as many people as possible to hear about me and what I do, people quickly turn away and the networking opportunity is lost.

Over the span of that two-hour reception, I met women from all walks of life–lawyers, administrative assistants, entrepreneurs, engineers, and CEOs. Most of the conversations were of the cocktail variety, but I left that evening amazed at the truth of the theory of six degrees of separation, which purports that everyone in the world is no more than six acquaintances from knowing anyone else. The statement "a friend of a friend" played itself out time and again with unpredictable connections.

During the chitchat at that influential cocktail party almost every person I met was connected to someone else I knew. We discovered mutual colleagues, a friend of a friend, and even distant relatives and former neighbors. As is so often the case, most people were connected by four or five degrees. By just showing a genuine interest in someone, the other person started to ask questions about what I did, which opened the door to talking about my coaching business and the benefits clients realize through coaching. This led to an exchange of business cards. Through follow-up, a number of those women have become clients or have recommended me to people in their network.

Coaching the Coach Tip

Marketing can be one of the more stressful aspects of having your own business. We often feel awkward about promoting ourselves as coaches and, as Christians, we may feel that we're guilty of pride when we tell others the benefits of our services. But if we strongly believe in the value of being coached, then we need to get past our discomfort of self-marketing.

I have shifted my thinking from marketing to networking. I have the God-given gift of gab. I am a people person and strongly enjoy meeting new contacts. I consider it a personal challenge to out-do my own level of friendliness. I realize other types of personalities are not as people-oriented as I am. But I believe that if my attitude shifts from marketing to networking, my goal will no longer be just to promote my own work but to create networks where opportunities exist for many to benefit.

When I network, one of my goals is to help the people I talk to become better connected than they were when we first met. This might translate into my being able to talk about my coaching services, but it could also mean that I am able to connect them with a colleague who deals more specifically with their needs. When I approach conversations with this other-centered attitude, I am not just looking out for myself but rather making the other person's needs paramount. Saying such things as "Have you ever heard about…?" or "I met someone the other day who was speaking about the same thing and they mentioned…." When we enter into conversations with this mind-set, people don't feel like we are self-promoting. Instead, they feel heard and believe that we care about them.

Our coaching skills give us the ability to ask good questions and draw out a person's dreams and values. Let's use these same skills to make connections and network with the people we encounter. In the long run we will all benefit.

Little gives me more pleasure than to help two strangers connect in a meaningful way that becomes a fruitful relationship, a strategic business contact, or a step toward significant life change. Just as in coaching, we don't create change. Rather, we become partners in effecting change. It's the same in networking. We help make connections that have the potential to effect change in other people's lives and in ours

---

1 http://www.sdpnonline.com/SDPN%20-%20Goals.htm accessed on September 5, 2012.

What Will Happen If You Don't?
Susan Whitcomb

For we are God's handiwork, created in Christ Jesus to do
good works, which God prepared in advance for us to do.
Ephesians 2:10

On a scale of one to ten, when it comes to love of coaching, I'm a ten. I love coaching others, I love being coached, and I love training others to become coaches. For me, coaching feels like I'm doing good works and walking in my Ephesians 2:10 gift: "created in Christ Jesus to do good works, which God prepared in advance for us to do."

It's a different story when it comes to marketing. On a scale of one to ten, I was about a three. I hated having to reach out and remind people about who I was, what I did, and the benefit I could bring to their lives with my services. This attitude cost me dearly, both emotionally and financially.

Early in my career as a budding coach, I mentor coached with Judy Santos, who has since passed away. Many consider her to be one of the most influential voices in the field of Christian coaching because she defined and moved the profession forward. At the time, she taught a foundational Christian coaching course that started me on the road to earning my credentials with the International Coach Federation. I knew I needed to be coached if I was going to be a successful coach, so she was a logical choice to be my mentor coach with her vast coaching experience and former business background.

We worked on a number of projects together, initially to help get my new career-coach-training certification program up and running. I'll never forget being just halfway into the four-month foundations class and announcing to her that I had decided to launch a career-coach-training school and teach others coaching. I could tell she was impressed with my enthusiasm but taken aback by, what I now label in hindsight, my naivety. I was a brand new coach; how in the world could I presume to train others when I'd been learning just a few months myself? But with the passion of a new convert, I just had to share the good news of coaching with my colleagues who were also career consultants.

I forged ahead. I loved developing the curriculum while getting the school up and running. I loved developing coaching techniques, wrestling with how to articulate the challenges people in career transition experience, and creating exercises to help others learn how to shift from career consultants and advisors into true career coaches.

Marketing always took a back seat. I didn't want to bother people. Able to see my blind spots better than I could, Judy would bring up the topic of marketing and ask what I was doing to market the program. I would respond with my list of excuses and what wasn't working: No one responded to my email campaign; I couldn't close the prospective student who had expressed interest in registering; I didn't have time to offer a free preview call to give people a taste test, and so on.

I was oblivious to my attitude about marketing and how it was impacting my success (or lack thereof) in the realm of bringing in new students. I procrastinated and rationalized and procrastinated and rationalized.

Judy used all the right coaching techniques. She looked at the root of my procrastination. We explored limiting beliefs around my marketing phobia, identified actions, and discussed the best methods for accountability, even agreeing at one point that I'd make a financial contribution to an organization that was against my moral values if I didn't follow through on my marketing commitments. All these things certainly created more awareness for me around marketing, but it didn't shift me into full-scale action.

Finally, one day Judy asked me about my least-favorite topic: "How's the marketing going?" I bemoaned my plight, replaying my favorite tape about the things I wanted to do, needed to do, but wasn't getting done. And that's when she asked me a question—the question—that has stayed with me and served me well for more than ten years: "What will happen if you don't?"

That question did what a powerful question should do. It took me into the future, made me examine my thinking, and shifted me into action. Since being asked that question, I have never thought of marketing in the same way. Now I no longer rate myself a three on that one-to-ten scale for marketing. It's more like a seven or even an eight, which is saying a lot for an ultra-sensitive introvert who still doesn't want to "bug people."

I now see marketing as an opportunity to love the people I serve, to offer them value in the midst of the marketing message, to inform them of new opportunities, and to remind them of the positive future they can create for themselves. And, yes, sometimes their future involves taking advantage of my services. I have come even to love the opportunity to market. The consequences of not doing so are dire, while the outcome of doing so brings blessing both to me as well as to the people I serve.

Coaching the Coach Tip

Do you dislike or procrastinate doing certain tasks in your life or work? What will happen if you don't do them? Step into the future and consider the consequences of procrastinating or doing them haphazardly. If the tasks are important to your success, how might you reframe each one so that you associate positive instead of negative thoughts with it? What might God's perspective be on this topic?

Is the task simply something that you don't know how to do well yet? (Remember that you can learn everything that's essential to your success.) If so, enlist in a course, mentor coach with someone who's mastered the task, or find an accountability partner who will help support you in the process. Perhaps you can explore ways to delegate the work, whether by paying someone or bartering the services.

Finally, reverse the question from "What will happen if you don't?" to "What will happen if you do?" Envision your world with that new task mastered, operating well, and bringing the results needed. What will be different? How will it equip you to serve the people God has called you to serve? How will it expand your reach, voice, impact, and territory? What do you think the Father would say to you when you've persevered and done this task with excellence? Remember that He is "able to do immeasurably more than all we ask or imagine, according to his power that is at work within us" (Ephesians 3:20).

You Can Promote Yourself
and Live to Tell About It!
Kathy Carlton Willis

Hide it under a bushel—NO! I'm gonna' let it shine.
"This Little Light of Mine" by Harry Dixon Loes

There are so many coaches doing what I do these days—how do I get more clients to even know my name so they can consider bringing me on to coach them?" Brad asked me this question at a recent coaching event.

"I want to reassure you that you can promote yourself and live to tell about it. You just need to study current marketing trends and select the ones that fit with your style and personality the best. There's no one right way to create buzz about your services."

Brad continued to look befuddled. "But it all seems so foreign to me. I just want to coach; I don't want to have to market myself. It doesn't come natural to have to hawk me to prospective clients. It makes me uncomfortable just thinking about it."

I patted Brad on the back and acknowledged his concerns. "What if I told you we can come up with a marketing plan that's painless? Well—almost. It takes work, but you can do it."

According to marketing research, it takes seven touches, on average, to convert a cold contact into any sort of yes response. For coaches, this yes means you gain new clients, and happy clients pass word along to others. Consider the following seven marketing techniques most likely to achieve positive results with the least amount of required resources. Implement them to expand your name recognition, extend your branding imprint, and see results.

1. Print Promotional Products

Use every outgoing piece of paper and every electronic document as business promotion. Consider including your contact info, logo, tagline, Web address, etc. Use on any business literature including business cards, business stationery, outgoing faxes, email signature line, and rack cards.

2. **Expert Articles**

Writing articles on topics related to your coaching expertise is an excellent business promotion technique. Many print and online editors need new materials all the time. Be sure to include your bio and your Web URL for additional exposure. Include a permission clause at the end to offer reprint rights to those wanting to share your content with their readers. Provide 400-word tutorials or columns as free article content for newspapers, trade publications, church-bulletin inserts, Internet sites (such as e-zines), newsletters and e-newsletters (e-blasts), guest-blogger posts, and document-sharing sites.

3. **Media Interviews**

Your local radio station or cable TV station needs to fill slots with guests for all their programming. Being interviewed is a great no-cost way to promote your business. Let the host know you're willing to share your expertise on a particular topic. Guest experts are always needed for popular call-in programs. Create a press release by connecting a hot topic to one of your passions, and send it to media contacts. Become the go-to person on certain issues that match your branding. To get a unique angle on the subject, members of the media like knowing which experts to contact as a story breaks.

4. **Seminar Presentations**

You have expertise in subjects of interest to others. You couldn't be in business if you didn't. Why not share that expertise through speaking seminars and promote your business at the same time? Offer some of your printed tutorials as additional resources, and be sure to incorporate your branding impression on all print literature you hand out to your classes.

5. **Social Networking/Word of Mouth**

Work to grow your contacts and content on social networking sites such as Facebook and Twitter. Contacts are the friends and followers with whom you interact. Content is any value-added posting you provide to your contacts. You will see a project have more of a ripple effect (which works like word of mouth) if you provide material they want to share with others. Provide links. Links are your friends.

6. **Audio and Video Clips**

    Once you've been interviewed by media, load the clips online to increase exposure. Make sure to get permission from the radio host or media outlet. Some media charge a fee to give you the rights to their program material. If the interview is archived on the media outlet's site, link to it from your website, blog, newsletter and social-networking sites. You can also capture audio and video from your speaking presentations to load online and link to them from your social networking sites.

7. **Cross-Promotion**

    What other influencers are reaching your target market? Write them to see about cross-promotional opportunities. Share links, resources, and endorsements. Offer to sell their products at your resource table if they will carry yours (and give an appropriate bulk discount or consignment deal). Write a guest article for their newsletters to gain exposure to new audiences. This can result in new clients.

Coaching the Coach Tip

The key for Brad, and any coach looking to market his services more, is to select options that make sense for your personality, your schedule, and your budget. How are you branding yourself? Branding includes:

- Your platform
- Anything you stand for
- Your issues
- Your image

- Your logo

- Your product

- Your messaging

Branding defines us—our "heart-core" messages. We all leave an imprint on others. Your brand is that overall impression you make (strategic) or leave (unintentional). No matter what, others make a decision about us based on what they observe. With that in mind, let's be deliberate with our branding. Does your branding match what you offer? If not, it's time to reevaluate. When you are true to you, that's the best brand of all, because it's the imprint God wants you to leave.

New to branding? Invite about a dozen people to be in your think tank or wisdom team. Make sure you include a variety of people who know you well (in the industry, in ministry, from your target clientele, loved ones). Conduct a survey. Ask them what key words best describe your essence. Pay attention to the common words that pop up on several lists. Try to capture those descriptor words in your brand.

Make sure your brand has a "deliverable" quality. Today's world has a "What's in it for me?" focus. Our clients have a consumer mentality even in selecting coaches, so be sure your brand tells them what they get when they choose you. Branding and marketing work together to help you spread the word about your services to the ones who need it most.

Be intentional to increase your exposure in order to maximize your opportunities. Rather than getting bogged down with a demanding marketing plan, focus on a strategic, step-by-step agenda. Instead of being overwhelmed trying to promote yourself, you'll be excited by the everyday ways you can interact with your target market. You can promote yourself and live to tell about it.

Market the Real You
Lisa Gomez Osborn

*The beginning of wisdom is this: Get wisdom, and whatever
you get, get insight. Prize her highly, and she will exalt you;
she will honor you if you embrace her.*
Proverbs 4:7-8 RSV

I read comments like this every day: "Achieve your dreams," "Believe
you can succeed and you will," "I coach others to reach their full
potential," or "Attend my tele-seminar for the ten secrets ...."

I'm not dismissing these statements altogether. In fact I've
written them or spoken similar things many times. However, there's
something amiss when the language used to communicate hope
and convey your unique strengths becomes so often repeated, with
the same or very similar vernacular over and over, that the message
begins to feel as genuine as a commercial for diet soda or laundry
detergent.

We are in the people-helping profession. When we lack
the enthusiasm and discipline to invest in our message, we can end
up sounding like a used-car salesman. I don't want that for myself,
nor do I want it for you. Therefore, we must intentionally choose
to be authentic and sincere when we communicate who we are and
what we know. People are turned off by the used-up jargon that is
redundantly reinserted into emails, ads, and social media. Be real.
People can smell disingenuousness from miles away.

When we use lingo, we de-value the Christian life coaching
profession. There is real potential for cheapening the profession
of life coaching and Christian coaching by the use of superfluous
coaching lingo. Let's put thought, energy, and passion into

communication about our careers that flows out of our personalities and a desire to serve Christ. When we continue to seek and to learn from credible and honorable sources, we acquire fresh and profound ways to express our distinctive gifts and personality.

I say all this foremost to myself. However, I believe this destructive trend demands our attention. If our genuine motivation is to help others through the truth of Christ and our professional strengths, then we must apply ourselves to the task wholeheartedly.

Something I spend considerable time teaching new coaches is how to locate and articulate their particular strengths and passions to their target market. I encourage them to take strength assessments such as Strengths Based Leadership 2.0[1] or Marcus Buckingham's "Now Discover Your Strengths"[2] as these both give new coaches a sound foundation from which they can begin searching for their own distinctive inspiration.

One of my coach trainees, Lindsay, has a natural strength labeled "activator." People with activator personality traits usually know how to makes things happen; they can quickly turn thoughts into action; they love making headway and change. Activator traits are great assets for you as a coach when your clients are stuck. Lindsay communicates this strength to potential clients by focusing and highlighting her skill as an activator in some of her marketing materials. She spotlights her coaching strengths to potential customers with something like "As a coach, I will give you support and keep you accountable. Together, we will create action-oriented solutions that will help you overcome the challenges you are facing and facilitate your forward momentum."

Anyone can take a strengths-assessment test. Even if we can't afford the assessment test fees, we can research different personality strengths and study their descriptions until we find five that match our own. We can pray for inspiration as we play with fresh ways to communicate our newly-discovered coaching strengths based on our personalities.

Yes, it does take more time than going online and copying and pasting someone else's material, but the time and effort you invest will produce an authentic message and a fresh approach to your marketing plans.

If you're a Christian coach or want to pursue this profession, recognize that you are responsible to those in your field and those you can influence to be ever-learning and ever-growing yourself.

Let's strive to be imaginative and reach deeply and prayerfully for newfound ways to communicate our distinctiveness to others.

Coaching the Coach Tip

As a Christian coach, you must do regular self-examination. Take the time and invest in learning more about your own personality and strengths through tests and assessments. In turn, the insight you gain will significantly help you effectively convey your aptitude and distinctiveness as a coach.

1 Rath & Conchie, *Strengths Based Leadership: Great Leaders, Teams, and Why People Follow*, Gallup Press, New York, NY, 2009.

2 Buckingham & Clifton, *Now, Discover Your Strengths*, New York, NY The Free Press, 2001.

Chapter 5

Providing the Structure

Analyzing the gap between where clients are now and where they want to go is an essential part of coaching. Equally important is providing the structure that will enable them to narrow that gap and eventually reach their goals.

In this chapter, our coaches share many ways you can help to provide that structure. We guide our clients as they establish their goals and determine what changes they are willing to make. We help them focus on the big picture and not lose sight of what's most important to them. We clarify what motivates and inspires our clients to stay on the path they have set for themselves. We assist them as they identify areas where they lack the internal structure necessary to produce real kingdom fruit. And we encourage them as they set clear boundaries to avoid being trapped by life's busyness and to work intentionally toward their goals.

Establishing Goals
Dr. Linda Mintle

If you don't know where you are going, you'll end up someplace else.
Yogi Berra

Julie first saw me on a national television show and decided I was the coach she needed. Given her initial goal for coaching, I wasn't so sure.

During our first visit, I asked her to fill out the requisite paperwork and tell me more about her goals for our coaching time. In a nutshell, Julie wanted to build a financial empire. Since I was not a financial coach and we were talking about a fairly large portfolio, I told Julie I was not the best person to help her reach that goal. When I suggested she employ a financial coach, she hesitated and insisted I be her coach. This began a discussion of what I could do for her based on my training and background.

What I could do was help her evaluate whether or not her goal was doable given her current life circumstances and life goals. Much in her life had changed since the time she was a major financial player in the business world. What I sensed from our conversation was her unrealistic expectation of what it would take for her to function in the business world like she did years ago. She was no longer a single woman who could work long and grueling hours, and she now had other responsibilities and interests.

For us to proceed, we had to agree on working goals. She began to articulate the challenge—reengage in the venture capitalist market with no sacrifice to her life balance. I didn't see how this was possible. She was now married with children, facts that did not exist when she made her first million. The hiccup in her proposed business success path had everything to do with the choices and changes in her life.

What I could do was help her evaluate the pros and cons of moving back into the world of high finance. What would it take, and how would her life be different? Was she willing to sacrifice areas of her life in order to reengage at her previous level of commitment?

Setting goals is the first and most powerful step in the coaching process. It is how progress and success are measured. Goals must be realistic and clearly defined by the client. Julie was asking to achieve a goal without considering the impact of that goal on other parts of her life. Her push to get back on top would come with a price to her family, personal leisure time, and friendships. Furthermore, in my opinion, her already problematic marriage needed more, not less, attention.

Her desire to have it all at this point in her life was unrealistic. Something had to give. Would it be her marriage, her children, her personal time, or her desire to be a financial player again? What part of her life would bear the sacrifice of time and attention if she reengaged in the financial market at the level she felt she needed to succeed?

Julie had to evaluate the amount of time and energy she could give to her career in order to duplicate her past efforts. So the agreed-upon goal of our coaching became a realistic reevaluation of what would change if she became a financial player again. Was she committed to that change, and would she accept the imbalance this would create in the rest of her life?

After several sessions, using the Wheel of Life tool, Julie had a better view of her life. She was able to consider each area—mother, wife, friend, community leader, and so forth—and assess the balance she currently had in each area against the balance she desired. Visually, she could see that she was already frustrated in certain areas due to her lack of time and attention. Adding her former business career to her current life would push more areas out of balance.

What Julie finally decided was to work on areas of imbalance and find a new way to engage in the business world, a way she could control and that would not require a huge investment of her time. Coaching helped her sort out her desires in a more realistic manner. She finished our sessions with a sense of what was possible in the here and now, developed goals for the future when her children were older, and initiated action steps that allowed her to keep her hand in the business world, making some deals but not going full-speed ahead at this stage in her life.

Once her goal was clear, the ambivalence she carried dissipated. Coaching helped her consider the impact of a desired change. At the end of our time, Julie was able to decide on a plan of action for now and in the near future.

Coaching the Coach Tip

Providing clarity about your parameters for coaching at the beginning of the relationship is important. Sometimes you have to challenge the validity of a client's goals and commitment. While being careful not to manipulate the person, you can be helpful by realistically laying out the consequences of various paths or choices. The earlier in the process you can do this the better the coaching will proceed. Goals direct the conversation and the action steps. When they are clear, the client can measure progress and make informed decisions.

Stonecutting or Cathedral Building?
Karen Porter

The LORD has made the heavens his throne; from
there he rules over everything.
Psalm 103:19 NLT

A well-known and often repeated story about construction goes like this. A traveler came across three stonecutters. Each was busy cutting a block of stone. The traveler asked the first, "What are you doing?"

The stonecutter answered, "I am cutting a stone!"

The traveler asked the second the same question.

"I'm cutting this stone to be sure it is square and uniform," he answered.

The traveler turned to the third stonecutter who seemed the happiest of the three. "What are you doing?" he asked.

The stonecutter replied, "I am building a cathedral."

Instead of working with stonemasons, I coach aspiring writers and speakers. My goal is for each client to learn the craft of writing so that writing well becomes natural and comfortable. I work with speakers to not only develop interesting and compelling content but also to improve the use of gestures, facial expressions, voice control, and body language. Along the way, we work on life issues, set goals, and dream big dreams. My greatest joy is to encourage a client to the point of seeing his or her eyes light up with hope and anticipation, or to shine a new light on a difficult situation, or to watch a dream take shape.

For instance, my client Lesli is a consistent and meticulous woman who never gives up her dreams even though life has handed her some big struggles. Family issues, the death of her mother, and infertility could have left her without joy or faith.

Lesli's dream of having children never came true. She did all the right things, followed doctors' orders, and pursued every medical option. Even though she is past the traditional age for childbearing, she believes in miracles such as happened to Sarah, Hannah, and Elizabeth in the Bible. Her faith is strong in the face of disappointment. Throughout her journey, a close relationship with God has helped her deal with well-meaning, but hurtful, conversations with people who don't really understand her struggle.

Before she came to me for coaching, Lesli had already begun a ministry to other women who are experiencing the pains of barrenness. Her group, Dancing upon Barren Land, is a vibrant ministry of one of the nation's largest churches, and more groups are forming in other cities. As she worked with this group of hurting women, she discovered the power and comfort and hope of praying Scripture. We began the process of putting these personal, beautiful, expressive prayers into a booklet format. We believe a woman who experiences the disappointment and frustration of childlessness will benefit from a purse-sized volume of Scripture-prayers when she feels angry or sad or when grief, jealousy, and fear overwhelm her. Lesli's prayers were authentic and powerful to other women because she lives in their same situation. All she needed from me was a little technical help with the writing craft and the flow of thought.

Still, I felt something about Lesli's journey was missing. Early one morning I spent a long time in prayer over Lesli and asked God to show me how to help her move forward to the greatness He had designed for her.

A few days later, we met to determine the next steps and future of the project. I sat back and observed Lesli as she read some of her work aloud. I saw a beautiful woman who appeared to have her act together on the surface. As she read, I heard the ache of her heart. Her disappointment and angst were tangible. I could feel her pain as her reaction to infertility hurt her to the core. Yet there was something else coming through the words and the way she expressed herself. I saw hope and peace.

I considered all the things I knew about her and how she worked through her discouragement and loss to find a way to help others. I remembered the months she worried over her mother's illness and her sorrow upon her mother's death. I recalled how the support of her five best friends (whom she calls her "five smooth stones") carried her through the ordeal. I reflected on her strong marriage and the entrepreneurial adventures she and her husband have embarked upon. I knew she was becoming a gourmet cook. I recalled that she and her friends had recently taken a girl's trip to New York City to explore and enjoy the sights. She had also shown me some new materials on teaching etiquette to children and corporate executives.

And then something amazing dawned on me, the coach.

She had already found the key to living with disappointments and pain. She'd kept moving and living and working and ministering even though her dreams were on hold. She didn't wallow in her pain; she lived while she waited.

As she finished reading, she looked up to find me smiling broadly.

"What?" she asked.

"Your prayers are beautiful, and I know they will be helpful to women who read your book, but I think you have something far more important to give to your readers. You need to write a chapter called 'Living Life to the Full while You Wait.'"

Lesli hadn't thought much about her accomplishments. She had considered her disillusionment and frustrations as failure and her goal was to cope, but her greater legacy is her ability to find joy, purpose, and influence despite her regret and disappointment.

Instead of merely surviving, she has blossomed into an encourager and inspiration to others. She didn't see it until I pointed it out to her that day. And I didn't see it until I stepped back from the details of coaching writing skills to see the big picture of her life.

Since then an amazing thing has happened to Lesli. She has new energy and vision for her ministry, but she also has begun to dream even bigger dreams beyond her original ideas.

As a coach, I didn't have a magic formula to help Lesli. In fact, I was focused on the skills, techniques, and methods of writing. I was looking at Lesli the stonecutter, if you will. But when I prayed and took time to observe and put all the pieces together, a new idea appeared. I saw Lesli the cathedral builder. When I communicated the idea to her, she was able to catch that vision of herself, too, and she was inspired and encouraged.

Coaching Lesli (and all my other clients) is more about developing life skills than writing or speaking expertise. Lesli still holds to her dream of bearing a child, and she still offers comfort and understanding to women. Now, however, she also encourages women to live to the fullest extent while waiting, to never let disappointment rule their lives, but to move forward with joy.

Coaching the Coach Tip

Whether we coach life skills, decision making, career moves, writing, speaking, business skills, spiritual disciplines, financial competence, family dynamics, or goal-setting, it is possible for us, as coaches, to focus too hard on the program and blueprint we have set out for our client. We can become a slave to the rubric, the step-by-step plan we have laid out. We get caught up in the process of mere stonecutting.

Sometimes coaching is about listening. To the client. To God. And sometimes coaching is about stepping back and putting all the puzzle pieces together to get a new perspective and panoramic view of our clients as cathedral builders. As a coach, I am learning not only to focus on the practical, mechanical techniques but also to take a long, broad look at the whole person. With a lot of prayer, God shows up with the right answer and lights the way for success. He is the God of the big picture. The heavens are His throne, and He sees the big picture. He sees the cathedral.

Motive-Based Coaching
the Key to Winning at Work
Dwight Bain

Do not be afraid. Stand still, and see the salvation of the LORD, which He will accomplish for you today...The LORD will fight for you....
Exodus 14:13-14 NKJV

What does it take to win at work?

People have asked me that question dozens of times after a keynote speech or radio talk show. Most likely your clients have asked you the same or similar questions. They want to know what action to take to build a successful life instead of being trapped in long-term failure. It's a great question. Unfortunately, since every person faces different challenges there isn't a 100-percent-specific answer that works for every person.

A better approach is to guide your clients in focusing on the real source of motivation by exploring their underlying motives. When you discover the motive behind why they want to win at work, you will be on track to help them shape a strategic approach to speed toward accomplishing goals and avoiding distractions that lead to failure.

Here are some key questions to ask your coaching clients:

- Do you want to win at work to deepen your resumè to advance your career?

- Does success at work mean making more money to bring home to your family?

- Does career success give you personal meaning and fulfillment?

- Does winning bring you a sense of satisfaction by proving you are the best?

Greater professional success usually gives a person far greater options in their personal life because increased income brings the flexibility to solve problems and control schedules by delegation. Outsourcing to save time and money is a wise use of resources. Working harder to gain greater self-esteem, however, is a dangerous motivator because it takes major sacrifices of time and energy and can often become a black hole of busy activity leading to workaholism.

Career burnout comes from attempts to fill up deep emotional insecurities through aggressive professional activity. Burnout won't lead to professional success and sadly is incredibly common among people who haven't seen the importance of mapping out a realistic career-coaching plan to win at work without losing at home.

Finding the Energy for Career Success

So how can clients stay motivated to achieve greater career success? Have them start by dealing with their core values, which can be identified through mapping out their internal motives, since motives lead to motivation.

Here are four key areas I use to inspire business professionals to stay focused to win at work while feeling greater energy and fulfillment in the process: insight, interests, importance, and identity.

Insight

There is a Scripture verse I was taught to pray every day: "If any of you lacks wisdom, let him ask of God, who gives to all liberally and without reproach, and it will be given to him" (James 1:5 NKJV). If you know that you don't know the answers, then asking for God's direction is a wise use of time. Generate insight by asking God to reveal your clients' special gifts and natural abilities, regardless of how much they may feel like they are struggling. Everyone has talent and ability at something. It takes insight to see it, and then it takes courage to stay focused to light the fire of desire in their heart, especially when you or they may feel like giving up. Have your clients enlist some of the people close to them, like a marriage partner, family member, or trusted friend to help them identify their talents and abilities if they don't already know them. Since these people already know so much about your client's personality, character, motivation, and inner drives, they will speak truth to that client.

Asking many questions to gain greater insight will protect against impulsive choices and ensure a greater likelihood of success. So don't be afraid to ask too many questions—of yourself or your clients—but do be afraid to stay silent on this important element.

Interests

Once your client knows his or her gifts, talents, abilities and skills, the next step is to see how those unique gifts could be transferred into something so incredibly interesting that the client wants to show up and learn more about it every day. There is an old saying that the curious are never bored, which is true. When your clients are inspired about pursuing something extremely interesting, they will lose all track of time because they are so engrossed. Linking their interests with greater insight leads to the next part of the process to win at work.

Importance

Once clients get inspired to pursue the aspects of their jobs or career callings that are most interesting, the next element to stir up personal motivation is to help them discover what is most important. What is valuable to them? What has great meaning? What activities or organizations do they believe in strongly? Everyone believes in something, yet many of us haven't taken time to explore and discover the core motives that fuel our desires to create positive change.

Now that you have mapped out the key areas that motivate people you are ready for your clients to advance to the final stage.

Identity

When people figure out who they are and what they enjoy doing, they are on track to live out their purpose and have more fun in the process. Perhaps the huge success of many work-related reality TV shows (like American Idol) is because they reveal what many people secretly would like their daily work experience to be—a place that allows them to utilize their creative abilities in an environment that rewards big risk-taking to achieve greater results. It's not hard to stay motivated when you know why you are going to work, and it's not hard to stay in the race to win, either. In fact, it makes it easier to move forward from a fear of failure with a new dedication to finish strong.

Avoiding Hidden Pitfalls

Now you and your clients have the basic career coaching strategies needed to win at work. Yet, even with these insights, many people are afraid to try and they often give up on the belief that they could have a better life by moving from what I call their day job over to fully experiencing their dream job. Why do they lack career confidence? Why are they still likely to fail? Three possible causes are that they are fearful, frustrated, or failing.

Fearful

Times are tough and many people are afraid about what the economy will do in the future. In fact, they can become so frozen in fear that they are afraid to try. It's normal to feel afraid, yet when you are overwhelmed with fear, it can often lead to becoming indecisive and totally zoning out. Since running away from reality feels easier than facing it for some people, they choose to stick their heads in the sand and completely deny what's happening to their industry. Think about how Blockbuster Video failed to make strategic changes with their customers and eventually filed for bankruptcy protection, while competitor organizations like Netflix and Red Box were thriving.

Some people retreat in a passive way and just slowly sink, while others try to avoid reality by using substances or media to escape. Avoiding major change by hiding in fear will lead to a major crisis. Being aware of these dangers and opening up the conversation with your clients by asking tough questions will help them protect themselves when they are heading toward a dangerous situation.

Frustrated

Clients often think they are frustrated with marriage partners or coworkers, but this pitfall is really more about them. Help them think about the times they were trying, but it just didn't come together. They knew they wanted to finish strong and have a meaningful career, but they felt like they lacked the horsepower to really pull out in front of the crowd.

When frustration builds up, it puts people at great risk because they face a tough choice: finish with mediocre results and risk getting laid off or downsized to try again at the next job, or just check out to avoid feeling the pain of not performing to their potential and quit. I've especially seen this with highly creative or bright coaching clients who procrastinated until the last minute and then couldn't finish projects assigned to them. Their frustration often comes out as anger directed toward the closest person to them. It's not fair, but it happens because they let the frustration take over, which blocks their ability to win at work.

Failing

Sadly, a failing, unmotivated person is the easiest to spot because they checked out a long time ago. When someone has reached this level, he or she is so unmotivated and gives up on even trying at the most basic of tasks, so his or her resumè just reflects a free fall down to zero. They totally and completely fail, which crushes their confidence. For many, failure kills the desire to try again, which leads many coaching clients to give up completely and drop out on the idea that a meaningful career was ever even a possibility. They are too depleted even to believe that God's promise spoken through the prophet Jeremiah, "Call to Me, and I will answer you, and show you great and mighty things, which you do not know" (Jeremiah 33:3 NKJV), is still available to them.

I challenge you to help such clients face their fears, frustrations, and the fear of failing with words of encouragement from God's Word. If they take time out daily to meditate on the Bible, I believe it will guide them from fear to greater faith by identifying their core motives, and then translating that into the powerful motivation needed to win at work.

Coaching the Coach Tip

You and your clients are stronger than you think, but just in case you are feeling beaten up by life, listen to the words of Moses in Exodus 14:13-14 (NKJV) as a final challenge when you or your clients are feeling unmotivated or scared about work or careers: "Do not be afraid. Stand still, and see the salvation of the LORD, which He will accomplish for you today.... The LORD will fight for you."

Life to the Full: Keys to Getting There
Dr. John Townsend

The thief comes only to steal and kill and destroy; I have come
that they may have life, and have it to the full.
John 10:10

The term "peak performance" is one of the applications of Jesus' statement, "The thief comes only to steal and kill and destroy; I have come that they may have life, and have it to the full" (John 10:10). Peak performance is fullness, the maximum good.

One of God's designs for us is to live out that fullness, and your coaching relationships are part of the process. Your clients need your help in experiencing that fullness, and this is the nature of peak performance. Helping your clients achieve peak performance is ultimately about two things: focusing on the spiritual fruit and the right path. Whether you are helping them with a business mission, life goals, relationships, or fitness or weight goals, these two aspects of coaching, done in God's way, cover the largest parts of their achievement.

Designed to Bear Fruit

Peak performance should lead to peak results, or good fruit. Clients want to get significantly better results with you than without you, and they are justified in this thinking. That means that there is what I call "double accountability." Clients must be accountable to you for the hard work that may be required, and you must also be accountable to bring about a return for their hard work. "Two are better than one, because they have a good return for their labor" (Ecclesiastes 4:9). You are both responsible for the results, together. So make sure you are focused on their goals at all times.

If you are a coach who goes deeper into your clients' lives, relationships, experiences, and issues, this can be a big help to them. For example, when the sales executive you are coaching can't make the sales she needs and you discover she has a fear of rejection, then you are beginning to help her in more of a holistic, whole-life way. At the same time, however, there is a danger in not paying attention to the result when you go deeper. Some coaches are more involved in the journey of growth and lose track of the measurable objectives of that journey. Too often, clients will do the same thing. They will be both engaged and encouraged about the deeper growth and lose clarity and focus. Your job is to keep the established coaching objectives in mind. So do both of these for your clients: Go deep and keep your eyes on the results.

The Path Itself

Peak performance also means your client is meeting his goals by going through the right process. It doesn't help him to achieve results by just any random method or shortcut. Cutting corners doesn't bring long-term transformation. People in weight training know that if you twist your body around to make that last repetition, it doesn't really help because the whole body is lifting instead of the specific muscle group they are trying to work. When the proper posture is used, however, the proper muscle group is isolated and stressed to the point of growth.

In the same way, clients will sometimes cheat without being aware of it. They will do their homework at the last minute, much the same way they did all-nighters in college. They start the process strong in the honeymoon period: Your coaching is the most important, hopeful, and wonderful thing in their lives! Then real life takes over; finances, work, parenting, relationship issues, and so forth, get in the way. Gradually, the coaching becomes less vital, especially if you don't pay attention to this dynamic. Instead, help them to stay the course. Work through the obstacles and issues, but don't get diverted. A lot of coaching is helping your clients learn to live like the ant: "Go to the ant, you sluggard; consider its ways and be wise! It has no commander, no overseer or ruler, yet it stores its provisions in summer and gathers its food at harvest" (Proverbs 6:6-8).

One reason clients have not reached their goals before meeting you is because they often have not created the internal structure necessary to stay the course. Accountability is necessary and vital. Accountability, however, has not done its work if your clients have not begun to internalize the structure of life that they need. For example, if after six months of coaching your client is still late to your meetings and doesn't complete agreed-upon assignments, then his life is telling you that the path is wrong. He may need to shift the focus to working on internal diligence. You may find that his success and fruit begin to increase just because you have helped his path in an area in which he was struggling and that was a source for other problems as well.

Peak performance is something you, as a coach, always need to keep in mind. Your clients will benefit from your help with their fruit and paths.[1]

Coaching the Coach Tip

Remember that helping your clients achieve peak performance is ultimately about two things: focusing on the spiritual fruit and the right path. Whether you are helping them with a business mission, life goals, relationships, or fitness goals, these two aspects of coaching, done in God's way, cover the largest parts of their achievement.

---

1 Re-printed from *Christian Coaching Today,* Volume 1, Issue 2 with permission of the American Association of Christian Counselors.

Busyness Versus Setting Healthy Boundaries
Denise Baumann

*"Martha, Martha," the Lord answered, "you are worried and upset about
many things, but few things are needed—or indeed only one. Mary has chosen
what is better, and it will not be taken away from her."*
Luke 10:41-42

Today's busy mom's number-one issue is with boundaries. It seems like time has slivered off an ever-shrinking calendar as we divide efforts between family events, school activities, after-school sports, work, and church. Often the first thing I hear from a mom in distress is "I'm so busy!" As her life coach, I think she has boundary issues.

A boundary "keeps the good in and the bad out" as defined in the book *Boundaries: When to Say YES, When to Say NO, to Take Control of Your Life* by Drs. Henry Cloud and John Townsend. This simple concept has great results when applied. The key to applying boundaries is to make sure that you have applied them to every area of your life, which oftentimes is easy to overlook. I wear more than one hat in my everyday life (woman, wife, mom, Christ-follower, and so forth). I apply boundaries to all the different hats I wear. Applying boundaries to include our different responsibilities allows us to live what we value every day. Setting boundaries allows us to manage our mental and physical limits. Often when we panic because we've overextended ourselves, we don't recognize our absence of healthy boundaries. Instead, we think we are just too busy.

To set some healthy boundaries as a coach, I start by asking my client how many "hats" (that is, how many responsibilities she has in her everyday life) she is currently wearing. Each "hat" comes with an expectation and a time commitment. I try to help the client recognize how many hats she is comfortable wearing. Some clients can wear many hats and thrive, whereas other clients thrive wearing far fewer hats. Identifying how many hats she can wear before it becomes detrimental helps us work together and be concise while setting boundaries.

Next, I add an experiential exercise by asking the client to fill out her version of a dream week on a blank calendar. On the same calendar, I have her fill in her actual commitments. Together we take a critical look at what absolutely needs to stay and what can go away. We try to look ahead and anticipate big events or things that have fallen through the cracks in the past. We also want to be sure to include family members and friends who may need to be a part of this decision-making conversation or process.

From this point on it gets fun. We start to put a plan in place (otherwise known as goal-setting) concerning where and when she will start setting boundaries. According to Hyrum Smith, "a goal is a planned conflict with the status quo." As my client and I set goals, we don't stop there; we also talk about the push back, or resistance, she will receive and put a plan in place for her response to that push back.

Maintaining good boundaries takes consistent attention. Each time my client and I meet, we review progress as well as how the current plan is working. Often it needs a little tweaking, so we make adjustments. I encourage my clients to use Sunday as their regrouping or reviewing day. By reviewing the previous week, we can see what worked and what didn't. According to Webster, knowledge, insight, and judgment are the foundations of wisdom.

When clients set and maintain boundaries correctly, they eliminate the overwhelming feelings of busyness that cause personal stress and block goals, which hinder them from attaining quality of life. When we stop sacrificing quality of life on the altar of busyness, we make boundaries our friend. We can live on purpose by having strong boundaries that maximize our efforts and energize our lives.

Coaching the Coach Tip

In my personal life I quarterly, or even seasonally, make a list of all the hats I am wearing to examine my busyness-versus-boundaries struggle. Once I've listed all the hats as well as expectations and time commitments, I look for balance. I try to follow Jesus' advice to Martha in Luke 10 by choosing the "few things" that "are needed." Since I am making an effort in my personal life to live my values, it is easier to come alongside clients to help them establish healthy boundaries. I have heard it said that just because you can doesn't mean you should. I would say, just because you can doesn't mean you are called.

Chapter 6

Gaining Clarity for Coach and Client

Clearly seeing things as they are is crucial for both the coach and the client. Knowing, however, that we all have blind spots, how do we as coaches see what it is we cannot see? One recommended way is to continue being coached by a professional who is willing to be honest and ask us the hard questions. Another way of banishing the blind spots is to seek the guidance of the Holy Spirit and to stay current about what's going on in our own hearts and minds.

We can help our clients gain clarity by using probing questions to help them discern between what they feel compelled to do and what is of lesser importance. Listening intently and using powerful metaphors are also extremely valuable in guiding our clients toward greater self-awareness.

Staying with the Questions
Anne Denmark

A plan in the heart of a man is like deep water,
But a man of understanding draws it out.
Proverbs 20:5 NASB

My coach, Susan, asked an important question: "How would you like me to work with you to address this situation?"

I knew what she was asking. Did I want a mentor from whom I could glean life experience, did I want her to advise me from her expertise and knowledge, or did I want to be coached? I am thankful she asked this question. It clarified things.

The focus of our coaching call was already firmly in place. My husband, Don, and I were flying back for the first time to a city we'd left six years earlier. It would be a quick two-day weekend to celebrate twenty years of ministry with a pastor and his wife from our former church. We were anticipating the reunion, yet the situation was complicated. We wanted to see many precious friends, but we had so little time. Susan and I decided to work out a plan for how Don and I could best maximize our brief visit.

I could have chosen to sort this out on my own, but I knew I would make wiser choices with Susan's support since my emotions were so involved in the trip. Having Susan's help would also speed up the process and keep me focused.

As I explained our situation, I could tell by her hmms and aahs that she was fully tracking my heart. She had recently relocated to another state and understood the intricate relationship dynamics of a return visit. It would have been so easy for her just to offer advice. Instead, she resisted. She remained in the coaching role by staying with the important questions. She asked, "How do you want me to work with you to address this situation?"

My answer was immediate: "I want to be coached." My heart was wrapped up in the people and the potential outcomes of the weekend. I didn't want advice or suggestions. I wanted to discover what made this a challenging return trip. I needed to chew over my own thoughts.

Susan didn't disappoint me. As she listened to me circling the issues, she kept me focused with direct statements such as, "You didn't answer the question." Her question challenged me to dive even deeper. Like a splash of cold water, her edgy approach jolted me into sudden self-awareness.

I resurfaced with a deeper understanding of how God wired me and of my deep need for these relationships. Susan patiently continued to draw out my answers and I was able to put a flexible plan in place. The process was exhilarating. The resulting reunion and celebrations were joyful.

I reflected on the importance of Susan's questions and the opportunity she gave me to discover my own answers. She truly demonstrated the skill of a masterful coach. She let me lead by determining the focus of our phone call and showed even deeper respect by allowing me to decide how I wanted her to walk beside me.

When you and I are coaching another coach, we are tempted to slip out of the coaching role and give advice. I know this. I coach other coaches. It is just too easy for you and me to give advice. We are constantly tempted to forget the transforming value of supporting our clients to work out their own answers. Perhaps something similar occurs when other professionals serve another in their profession. The relationship can become skewed or perhaps a little uneasy like a doctor treating another doctor or a hairstylist cutting another stylist's hair. The underlying truth is I know that they know what I know.

I believe every coach needs a coach. It keeps us sharp. After eight years in the coaching profession and now teaching coaches, I still need a coach. The longer I coach, the more I need a coach. Having my own coach brings me back again and again to discovering the value of coaching. And a big part of coaching is the coach's ability to stay with the questions while the client does the work of self-discovery.

Just the other day my client Linda, who is also a coach, established the focus of our call on physical exercise. Immediately, my mind raced with quick tips from my own personal experience. There I was again at the familiar decision-making crossroads. Do I give advice or stay in the questioning mode so that she may make her own discoveries? Thanks to my own recent experience with my coach, I chose the latter.

At the conclusion of our call Linda said, "Wow! You are really good." Actually, she did the really good work and all I did was stay in the coaching role, stay in the question mode, and allow her to discover her own answers.

It is scary to think after all these years how tempted I still was to offer suggestions instead of offer the transforming gift of discovery. I still need a coach. How about you? How often are you tempted to give advice instead of the gift of discovery?

Coaching the Coach Tip

Jesus asked simple, powerful, and timely questions. He wanted you and me to think, to examine, and to discover the deep places of our hearts. He was the masterful coach.

For years, I've posted helpful coaching models, quotes, and lists on my office bulletin board. With a quick glance, I can scan the richest contents of my coaching toolbox. One of my favorites is this one by Jimi Hendrix: "Knowledge speaks but wisdom listens."

Jesus was wise. He asked powerful questions so He could listen to people's hearts. But let's face it. He already knew what was in their hearts. He asked those questions to help people understand their own hearts and gain wisdom.

When you and I coach, we frequently find ourselves at the crossroads of choosing between giving knowledge through advice or giving the gift of self-discovery through questions. I am sure you know this crossroad well. Be wise. Help your client hear his or her own heart by staying with the questions.

Paying Attention to Your Life
Dr. David Stoop

Pay close attention to your life.
1 Timothy 4:16 ISV

It's difficult to foster self-awareness in our clients if we as coaches haven't been willing to walk down that path ourselves. Because we bring our own stuff into our coaching sessions, either intentionally or unintentionally, it's important to stay current with what's going on in our own hearts and minds.

The apostle Paul, who was what you could call a coach, instructed Timothy, his coachee, to pay close attention to his life. One way to do that is to ask yourself some powerful questions. Here are a few questions that have helped me stay objective about my life.

Am I Paying Attention to What Is Impacting Me Emotionally?

I was working with a grieving widow whose husband had died in a plane crash. She had shared how their last conversation just before he boarded the fatal flight had been filled with anger. We had talked for a number of sessions and she seemed stuck in the grieving process. Finally the breakthrough came as she blurted out, "I was so angry that I didn't tell him I loved him at the end of the conversation!"

That conversation left me with a deep sadness. Later, as I reflected on her story, it hit me how much was left unfinished in her life. Her father wouldn't let her see her husband's body, and she hadn't gained closure on their last disagreements. Naturally, I started to wonder what was unfinished in my life. What had I left undone or unsaid in my closest relationships? If I was to die suddenly, would my wife know that I had loved her?

Am I Making My Closest Relationships a Priority?

As a marriage and relationship coach, I encourage my clients to invest time with those they love, knowing how those closest connections are key to a meaningful life. If I am staying current in my marriage, then I need to ask myself routinely if I am making my wife a priority.

One thing my wife and I have found especially helpful in building intimacy in our marriage is to pick ten or twelve verses in Scripture to focus on. We each read the assigned verses separately, paying special attention to what the Holy Spirit might be revealing. After we have read the verses several times, we each journal our thoughts or insights. Later, we sit down together and share what God has shown us. At the end of our discussion, we take five minutes for meditative prayer.

This small investment of time not only helps us to grow closer but to stay current with what each of us is thinking and feeling. In addition, our ritual is a way of making our marital relationship a priority as well as deepening our relationship with God. And that leads me to the next question I ask myself.

Am I Paying Attention to Growing Emotionally and Spiritually?

What am I doing to nurture my emotional and spiritual growth, or am I just expecting it to happen? If my faith as a Christian is a core value of mine, then am I intentionally shining God's light in the darker areas of my heart? Maybe there is a grudge or some unforgiveness I need to deal with. Or perhaps there is some pride or arrogance I'm justifying or tolerating.

I see people who are so caught up in the busyness of their lives they have no time for reflection on their own life. I saw a couple last night. He works probably sixty hours a week, travels often in business, and even when he is home for a short time, his Blackberry is in his hand and he is still "at work." Sometimes in the middle of their conversation, his wife begins to talk about the "circus that came to town and the elephants in their yard." As she suspected, he wasn't hearing a word she said. If he couldn't listen to his wife, you know he is not listening to his own emotional or spiritual needs.

Am I consistently carving out the time needed for self-examination? Or am I slowly drifting away from this routine? We hold our clients accountable for the actions they want to take. Who is holding me accountable to follow through?

Coaching the Coach Tip

Stay current, or pay attention, in your own life by taking time for self-reflection. What is impacting you emotionally this week? If you look at how you recently have spent your time and resources, would that reflect the priorities you say are most important? What are you doing to intentionally grow emotionally and spiritually? Is there someone who is paying attention to your life and holding you accountable to do what you said you wanted to do? Remember, we cannot successfully encourage our clients to pay close attention to their lives if we aren't willing to do the same ourselves.

What Could You Not Do?
Martha K. Greene

We feel concerned about a lot of things, but not compelled by them.
Gary Barkalow

A dear friend back East sent me an email about the possibility of coaching a friend of hers. Her description of him included the words "amazing," "excellent," "communicator," "leader," "giftedness," and "value," all of which, I was soon to learn, were spot-on descriptions of her friend, Michael.

I promptly sent Michael a letter explaining what coaching was all about and invited him to have a free discovery call with me to see if he and I were a good fit. He replied immediately, saying he was "very excited" to talk to me about life coaching. After our call, he hired me as his coach.

When I received the client information from Michael's welcome packet, I knew I had embarked on an E-ticket ride. (For those born after 1982, E-tickets were for Disney's newest and most thrilling rides). Michael had more passion-filled dreams than Methuselah could have had in his 969 years.

Over the weeks that followed, Michael unpacked his dreams—both the ones he had given up on and the ones he wanted to pursue. I was thrilled to have a client who was so future-focused, so eager to grow and change, and so committed to using his gifts for God's kingdom and glory. Prayerfully and carefully, we worked together as Michael defined and refined his dreams.

About six months into coaching Michael, something unusual happened in one of our sessions. Typically, I almost had to interrupt him to ask him one of those powerful questions coaches ask to create awareness for their clients. Since it was the beginning of the year, I persevered and asked, "A year from today, what would you want to have happened in your life?"

"I would…" He hesitated.

"I don't know…" He stopped, silent.

"I need to have…" Again silence.

And finally, he said, "I want to have …"

He had been neither hesitant nor silent in any of our other sessions. It was an ah-ha moment for me. I remembered something I had heard as a child: "It doesn't matter how big your bucket is, just carry it full." The only problem with that seemingly sage advice is, if your bucket is big, and you get it full, you can't carry it. Michael's bucket was big, and it was full. No wonder he couldn't answer my question. While perusing my notes before our session, I had noticed a comment he had made early on: "I sometimes feel my dreams are unattainable because I have so many."

Our clients are so wise. As coaches, we need to actively and attentively listen to them. I was delighted to be coaching someone who was so capable and dream-driven that I failed to notice he was drowning in his giftedness and exhausted from lugging his big bucket of dreams around.

In my desire to better coach Michael, I pulled out some material on the topic of one's calling, and I came across this quote from author and speaker Gary Barkalow: "We feel concerned about a lot of things, but not compelled by them!" Later, when I shared Barkalow's quote with Michael, I asked, "What could you not do?" He was again hesitant and silent. It was an ah-ha moment for him. This question was the sifter he needed to catch those things that he was not just concerned about but compelled by.

Over the next few months, Michael took the Strength Finder 2.0 assessment, which confirmed his gifts. He also polled friends about what they felt his most unique quality was—which was an additional confirmation of his gifts. He made a move to be closer to his job; he changed positions within his company; he applied to, and was accepted for, graduate school; and he is currently halfway through his master's program.

Throughout our coaching process, Michael continued to seek the Lord. God has honored Michael's seeking and has stretched and grown and matured him in marvelous and miraculous ways. As I have coached Michael, God has done the same thing for me. The coaching relationship changes not only the client but also the coach with God's amazing grace lavished on both.

Michael still dreams big, but he only puts into his bucket what he is compelled by and what he can carry. I have no doubt he will arrive at home plate as humorously described by Hunter S. Thompson: "Life should not be a journey to the grave with the intention of arriving safely in a pretty and well preserved body, but rather to skid in broadside in a cloud of smoke, thoroughly used up, totally worn out, and loudly proclaiming, 'What a ride.'"

I'm thankful Michael has let me take this E-ticket ride with him for a season as his coach. I can't wait to see what God has for him down the track. I expect to hear him proclaiming, "Wow!" all the way.

Coaching the Coach Tip

The coaching relationship is a unique one, and as coaches we have a unique opportunity to travel with and influence our clients during a stretch of their life journeys. The clients who come to us are all gifted by God. Many are multi-gifted. You may have had, or may someday have, a client like Michael. In your delight at having such an ideal client and your enjoyment of helping that client express and capture his or her dreams, don't overlook that the dreams can become a distraction or possibly a detriment. The reality is the dreams may be weighing him or her down. Help such clients discern what they are compelled by and to put that in their buckets.

As Christian coaches, we have the Holy Spirit to give us insight and wisdom. Praying before each session opens us up to the Spirit, and praying with the client invites Him into the coaching session. For me, especially as a relatively new coach, prayer has been invaluable. I have also found it invaluable to have a coach myself. It is the best way to become a better coach.

Styles of Communication
Georgia Shaffer

You will be blind to some things in your interactions with your clients.
Darren Dahl

An essential part of having self-awareness as a coach is not only to have clarity about your personality, your strengths and weaknesses, but also to have clarity about your style of communicating. For example, some of us tend to be direct and to the point when interacting with our clients. Others are easygoing. We listen, watch, and ponder before speaking. Those of us who have the detailed organized personality have a deeper, more deliberate, way of expressing ourselves; whereas, the high energy outgoing type of person loves to talk and often thinks out loud, bouncing ideas off others.

I find the easiest way to understand the communication styles is to understand the different personalities. While there are many personality assessments on the market today, such as Myers Briggs Type Indicator (MBTI) and the DISC, to help you understand your style, I'll reference the personality assessment designed by Florence and Marita Littauer in their book *Wired that Way*. The names of the different personalities they use are Popular Sanguine, Perfect Melancholy, Powerful Choleric, and Peaceful Phlegmatic.

Popular Sanguine

The Popular Sanguine is the high energy outgoing person who loves to talk and tell stories. Their desire is to have fun and be entertaining even if that means they look silly or make jokes about themselves doing it.

Their style of communicating is to think while speaking and sometimes to speak before thinking. If this is your personality, then you are gifted in people skills. As a coach you can not only make clients feel comfortable but you are great at motivating and inspiring them.

As a Popular Sanguine coach, however, you need to guard against dominating the coaching session. While you are creative, love to brainstorm, and hate dead air, you will need to learn to get comfortable with pauses. Watch what happens when you create open spaces in your sessions. Be aware and ask yourself, is my client doing most of the talking?

As a Popular Sanguine coach you can think on your feet. A danger, however, is that as a coach you can respond too quickly. Don't necessarily say the first thing that comes to your mind. Filter it through by asking yourself, will this question or comment I am about to make be helpful or harmful to my client?

Perfect Melancholy

The total opposite of the Popular Sanguine in communication style and personality is the Perfect Melancholy. They are the thinkers, tending to be more thoughtful and deliberate in their communications.

Their basic desire is for perfection and organization. The Perfect Melancholy coach can see the details that are critical to a project or a client's goal. But that doesn't mean that you need to overwhelm your client with all that you see. Guard against getting too intellectual or focusing on too many of the facts and figures.

The Perfect Melancholy is gifted in analyzing and helping clients break down a goal into doable steps. If this is your personality ask yourself, am I listening intently to what the client is saying or am I overanalyzing the situation and maybe making incorrect assumptions? Because being flexible and going with the flow can be challenging for the Perfect Melancholy who likes to create a plan and then implement the plan, you will need to remember that some of the personalities are not as organized as you are.

Powerful Choleric

The Powerful Choleric personality is the doer, the just-get-it-done kind of person. Their style of communicating is to be direct and to the point. Their basic desire is for control.

As a coach, the Powerful Choleric has a tendency to think they know what should be done, who should do it, and how it should be done. While you may think you have correctly assessed a situation, remember it is only your opinion and you don't want to tell your clients what you think they should do as only God knows what is best for them.

As a Powerful Choleric, you love challenges and are willing to confront problems everyone else wants to run from. What may be difficult for you, however, is to remember your role as a coach is not to fix things. One Powerful Choleric coach who realizes her tendency to do that said, "I need to remember that it is far better to listen. When in doubt, I don't say whatever it is I might be wondering if I should say."

Peaceful Phlegmatic

The Peaceful Phlegmatic is the laid back, easygoing personality. If this is your personality, you don't like to make waves because your basic desire is for peace and quiet. Your style of communicating is to watch, take things in, and ponder them for awhile.

Coaches with the Peaceful Phlegmatic personality bring a sense of calmness even in the midst of a crisis. They naturally bring a soothing touch and a cooperative spirit into a session.

Since you like to ponder things, you might be too hesitant to make a comment or help a client verbalize what they are thinking or feeling. One problem I have often heard from Peaceful Phlegmatic coaches is, "I don't feel like I have anything valuable to contribute." As a coach, ask yourself, am I actively interacting and engaging with my client?

Also realize as a Peaceful Phlegmatic coach, you might have the tendency to push things under the rug. You might be afraid to mention something or confront an issue that needs to be addressed. Have confidence in your abilities to collaborate and add value to the client.

Although you may not choose to use any of the personality inventories with your clients, it's still important for you as a coach to have a basic understanding of the different personalities and how each prefer to communicate. Regardless of the personality names and categories you are familiar with, remember to respect all communication styles.

Coaching the Coach Tip

Take a moment and decide on your style of communication. Do you like to interact with your clients in fun and creative ways, in organized and precise ways, the only way (your way), or the easy, relaxed way? Give yourself and your clients permission to communicate the way God created each of you.

If you are having problems deciding what your personality and your style of communicating is, then ask yourself which of the styles feels most comfortable to you? Which one is your natural, shoes-off self? Observe yourself in different settings, and pay attention to how you naturally express yourself.

Most of us tend to be a blend of two different personalities. For me as a combination of a Powerful Choleric and Perfect Melancholy, that means I will tend to be direct and detailed in my interactions. A Popular Sanguine and Peaceful Phlegmatic coach, on the other hand, will bring energy and enthusiasm as well as a cooperative spirit.

If you are still stuck, then you may find it helpful to ask several people who know you well and who you trust which personality they think describes you best. If they all say, for example, that you are definitely the Peaceful Phlegmatic, then be willing to hear what they are suggesting. Although you might not be able to see everything about the way you interact and communicate with your clients, don't let lack of awareness about your general style of communicating be one of those blind spots.

Am I Taking Time To Listen?
Nancy Williams

Seek first to understand, then to be understood.
Stephen R. Covey

A psychologist thought he had cleared his calendar for an extra day to rest after his vacation. While he was relaxing in his office, a patient came to his door.

"Hello, Doctor. I'm glad you're back."

A bit startled, the psychologist realized he had not changed the woman's appointment time. Although he was exhausted, he could tell she was troubled, so he welcomed her in. The client poured out her heart as he struggled to focus.

When the hour ended, the client gathered her things, and said, "Thank you, Doctor. Same time next week?"

"I'll see you then," he replied as they walked to the door. Embarrassed and disappointed in himself, he tucked her check into her file. I feel terrible, he thought. I know I wasn't very attentive or helpful. I'll hold her check until next session and apologize. Hopefully, she'll understand.

When the same client arrived for her next session, he prepared to do just as he planned.

Before he could begin his apology, she spoke. "Doctor, I want to talk about last week's session. How did you know that was exactly what I needed?"

A bit surprised and very relieved, he responded, "Please tell me more."

"I needed someone to simply listen. I didn't need explanations or lectures or criticism. I just needed a quiet, safe place to vent and someone to listen without interruption. And you did just that. By the end of our session, I was able to think about things more clearly. I took some positive steps this week and feel much better. Thank you."

The psychologist smiled as he quietly tucked her check back into her file. "Great. Let's continue."

I heard that story during one of my classes as we talked about the value of listening to clients. While I don't endorse being inattentive or uninvolved when working with clients, the story does reflect the importance of giving time and space for clients to share.

Listening is perhaps the most important tool we can use as coaches—listening to what our clients say and what they don't say, listening to ourselves as we consider our work with them, and listening to God.

While I know listening is important, I also know how easy it is to jump right in with tools to address presenting issues. I want to help clients move forward and reach their goals. They are often looking for quick solutions, and I want them to be successful. So it's easy for me to feel that same sense of urgency, especially if I have other clients with similar goals.

When I began coaching, I focused a lot on assessments, forms, and various tools to guide the coaching process. I was eager to use all available resources to help clients move forward. I wanted to be ready to roll up my sleeves and get right to work with them on designing the futures they envisioned.

These elements of the coaching process help gather information and provide structure to assess needs and design action plans. I've also learned the value of allowing time for a client to share his or her unique story early in the coaching relationship and to ask questions that open the understanding to look deep within to find passions, desires, experiences, and fears. I actively pay attention to what my clients are saying and then encourage them to listen to themselves and to God as they consider how to meet their goals and realize their dreams. As we do this, they often recognize that their relationships are deepened and they may uncover hidden roadblocks and concerns that could potentially prevent them from moving forward as they desire.

Early in my coaching experience, I worked with Karen, who had recently moved from another location, on a new business venture she wanted to pursue. She had dreams and ideas but was struggling with focus and structure to implement her plans. She was scattered and easily overwhelmed. Karen is a capable, experienced, successful businesswoman who felt frustrated.

"I feel like I'm spinning my wheels and getting nowhere," she shared during our first session. "I should be managing life a lot better. I'm failing at something I should be able to accomplish. So I need your help to get focused and organized."

I sensed there were factors she had not shared that might be hindering her from moving forward. I suggested we set aside the business plan for a bit and talk about the bigger picture. I began asking about her life before her recent move. I felt I was tapping into a place Karen didn't want to go, but I gently pressed, sensing we'd uncover a source of her frustration.

"My husband filed for divorce a year ago after twenty-six years of marriage. I didn't see it coming, and I've had a lot to deal with because of him. But I refuse to let that get me down. I'm here, I'm fine, and I'm starting over. So we don't need to talk about it."

Her words communicated one message; her tone and body language spoke quite another. I made a comment about the grief that comes with divorce and asked how she was mourning the losses she faced and adjusting to her subsequent move.

She responded quickly, saying, "I don't have time for that."

While I wanted to jump right in with my opinions, God prompted me to "be quick to listen, slow to speak" (James 1:19). So I remained silent and she soon began to open doors within herself that had been tightly closed.

As she shared and I listened, it became apparent that her unaddressed grief was weighing her down, keeping her from the clarity she needed to engage fully in her new business venture. We both recognized wounds that needed healing in order for her to move forward and create a fresh start both personally and professionally.

She talked about her struggle with praying yet finding roadblocks at every turn. Again, my instincts were to respond right away, but I let my silence open a door. And I listened.

She said, "Maybe all this time God has been telling me to take time to heal before jumping into something new."

As our work together continued, God guided Karen through a time of transition and prepared her for a fresh start. In His timing and according to His plan, doors began to open toward her professional goals, and she's now on her way to achieving her dream.

Coaching the Coach Tip

It's important to equip ourselves to help our clients achieve their goals. God wants us to be good stewards of the talents, training, and resources He has given us. He has also shown me the importance of taking time to listen fully to the hearts of my clients, to listen to Him as He guides the coaching experience, and to follow as He leads, even when it means setting aside my plans and agendas.

As I prepare to meet with clients, a Bible verse I prominently display in my office becomes my daily reminder. Perhaps it will serve as a guide for you as well. "Trust God from the bottom of your heart; don't try to figure out everything on your own. Listen for God's voice in everything you do, everywhere you go; he's the one who will keep you on track" (Proverbs 3:5-6 THE MESSAGE).

When Reality and Client Goals Collide
Mary J. Yerkes

But speaking the truth in love, we are to grow up in all
aspects into Him who is the head, even Christ.
Ephesians 4:15 NASB

Allan tried to steady his voice as he spoke. "How do I get my health under control so I can go back to work?"

A former Marine and decorated Army officer, he had served his nation with dedication and excellence, completing demanding missions while ensuring the welfare of the soldiers entrusted to him. Strong Christian character and such values as self-discipline, motivation, and confidence made him a standout both on and off the battlefield.

When Allan first contacted me, he was facing his most formidable enemy yet—advanced Lyme disease. Transmitted by infected ticks, Lyme disease can be severe and debilitating, resulting in neurological disturbances including cognitive dysfunction, memory loss, and temporary paralysis. Allen saw his illness as just one more obstacle to overcome, and he was looking to me to guide the process of moving toward his desired goal—to return to work.

During our initial sessions, Allan needed to vent, or "clear" the situation, pouring out his pain and frustration. I paraphrased and mirrored back to him what he said to ensure that I understood, listening not only to his words but also to his heart. He was frightened by the thought that he might not be able to provide for his family.

Knowing his faith was strong despite his illness, I felt he needed help reframing his situation to see it from God's perspective.

"Allan, you are a committed man of God, and I admire your strength and faith in the midst of a very difficult situation. You have told me what your goals are. How can you engage God in this situation and discern His goals and agenda for you?"

"I didn't think of that," he replied.

I responded with inquiry questions:

- What if God is leading you in a new direction for this season of life that doesn't include returning to work?

- How would that affect how you view your current situation?

Allan agreed to consider these questions in the days and weeks ahead. He spent many hours wrestling with God in prayer and Bible study, although answers were neither quick nor easy.

A few weeks later, my heart leapt as Allan said, "I've not wanted to admit it, but I can't return to work. After praying about it and talking with my wife, I've decided to file for permanent disability."

I expected his decision would be freeing, that he would feel a weight lift from his shoulders. Why then did his voice ring hollow? The answer, his unspoken concern, lay beneath his words: What now? How will I provide for my family? I've spent almost my entire adult life in the military. What is God's plan and purpose in my life now?

I coached Allan for the next nine months, and he overcame many obstacles, working hard to define a new normal and find new purpose in this new season of life. As his health waxed and waned, both he and I battled frustration.

Allan ultimately stopped coaching, not because he was not benefiting from the process but because he could no longer afford it. I struggled, feeling as if I somehow failed him. My perspective, however, shifted several months later when I read an excerpt from his testimony which he had written for a ministry newsletter:

Having been a Marine and an Army officer for many years, I can say that the elite military units are subjected to the most difficult and dangerous training. The training I went through with the Marine Corps, then Army Airborne (parachute) training, and Army Ranger training was tough. But such training is vital to prepare those elite military personnel for their duties, which far exceed what the average soldier, airman, or Marine is called to do. So I like to think that those of us whom God has "blessed" with particularly difficult circumstances are those who have a special calling—such as providing informed comfort to others who are suffering.

While frustration with his physical limitations was evident, his faith was strong and his focus was toward the future.

Was Allan's coaching a success, even though he didn't achieve his initial goal? I believe that it was. Although Allan failed to meet his goals, he embraced God's purposes for his life. What better outcome could a Christian coach and client hope for?

Coaching the Coach Tip

Perhaps you have a client like Allan, one who has hired you to support his goals, but his agenda is unattainable.

In cases like these, the coaching skills of creating awareness and direct communication are especially important. As a coach, I had a strong opinion about what might be the right course of action for Allan. I recognized, however, that I would do my client a disservice by injecting my advice into the conversation and short-circuiting his discovery process. Not letting myself be swept up in his emotions, I instead chose to let him work through his own process.

Because of his strong Christian faith, I was able to challenge him to seek God's perspective on his failing health. While listening to his concerns I did not allow his perspective to hook me. Instead, I used powerful questions to stretch him and help him gain greater understanding and self-awareness.

In his book *Coaching Questions: A Coach's Guide to Powerful Asking Skills*, Tony Stolzfus suggests several questions to help a client identify a blind spot:

118

- Let's say this situation is custom-designed to prepare you for what you were born to do. How would that change your perspective on your circumstances?

- What is the opportunity here? How can this move you toward your destiny?

- What do you want to admit to yourself about how you are making this choice?

In addition to powerful questions, metaphor and analogy are helpful to paint a picture. For example, in coaching clients like Allan, I might use a military metaphor or analogy and ask a question such as, "If you were to see God as the officer in charge and yourself as a soldier under His command, what steps might He take to ensure your welfare during this difficult time? How might that apply to your current situation?"

The ways to work with a client are endless. But remember, while strong coaching competencies are critical for success, walking in lockstep with God's Spirit yields eternal fruit and rewards for your clients and for you.

Chapter 7

Fostering Self-awareness in Clients

Self-awareness is one of the four foundational competencies of emotional intelligence and impacts every aspect of our clients' lives. Research has shown that in a work setting, 83 percent of the top performers rate high in self-awareness, while only 2 percent of bottom performers have a high level of self-awareness.

We can foster self-awareness in our clients by accepting them for who they are so that they will be more willing to take an honest look at the unflattering parts of themselves. Another way is to guide our clients to identify their essence: What shows up when they walk into a room? Helping them to identify their personality along with their strengths and weaknesses promotes self-awareness. By identifying the critical voices that sabotage them while focusing on God's truth, they can experience the kind of success God has designed for them.

The Proverbs Project
June Hunt

The one who calls you is faithful and he will do it.
1 Thessalonians 5:24

Years ago I had the privilege of staying in the home of a highly respected couple during a week-long speaking and singing tour. Steve, Shelly, and their daughter Courtney couldn't have made me feel more at home.

I arrived in Orlando on a Friday and needed to travel to West Palm Beach the following Friday for a television appearance. As it turned out, Steve had business to conduct in West Palm that very same Friday, so when he offered to drive me there and back, I was delighted. During the three-hour trip, Steve and I chatted about numerous topics—from current events to the economy to his job. But within the first twenty minutes, the conversation dove into the deepest of waters.

"June," Steve said somewhat hesitantly, "I wonder if I could talk to you about a problem I've been struggling with for a long time."

"Absolutely! I'd be honored to help in any way that I can."

"It's my anger. No matter how hard I try, I just keep failing. I feel so guilty, especially because of the toll it takes on my family. Shelly is a wonderful wife. I couldn't ask for more. We've been married for twenty-six years, and she has been so patient with me about this. But I know I've hurt her many times by the way I've exploded when I'm mad. It's as if everything I know in my head flies right out the window. And to see the look on Courtney's face after I've yelled about something I should have handled so much differently...I feel like such a failure. Do you have any ideas?"

I was impressed with Steve's humility and authenticity. Though he was a successful businessman, respected church leader, and devoted family man, he knew he had a problem. He seemed genuinely ready to change. What Steve did not know was that gracious Shelly and Courtney, each separately and privately, had mentioned Steve's anger to me earlier in the week—completely unprompted. I didn't divulge this to Steve, but the unified message was clear: Anger kept him from reaching his God-given potential.

Immediately, I felt impressed to present Steve with a project. I asked, "Would you be willing to embark on a project for one month to address your anger?"

"Yes, I would," he replied without hesitation. "What is it?"

"Would you be willing to read one chapter of Proverbs each day for a month?"

"A chapter a day? That's it?"

"Well, begin with chapter one and read each verse slowly so the words sink into your mind and heart. Then, each day, write down every verse that has anything to do with anger, whether speech or attitude. When you're finished, review the verses you've written and ask the Lord what He wants you to learn from them."

"Sure," he said. "I can do that. No problem."

We dubbed our experiment "The Proverbs Project."

On Saturday, I returned to my home in Dallas, praying during and after my flight for God to work powerfully in Steve's life. For the next eight weeks, I heard nothing from him. Then, at the beginning of week nine, I received the following note:

Dear June,

I'm a changed man. Every morning after breakfast, Shelly and I read a chapter in Proverbs. At first, I thought, "Why did June give me the project—nothing I've read has anything to do with anger?" But I stayed with it and completed The Proverbs Project.

When I read all the verses that show what an angry man looks like, I was overwhelmed by the image of the person

I did not want to be—someone who stirs up strife and dissension, someone people should avoid. I knew I needed to change. Well, bottom line—the Lord is changing me.

A short time later, I had dinner with Shelly and Steve, who were in Dallas on business. What a delight to hear how God had worked. Not only did Steve note the change, but also Shelly was quick to confirm, "The Proverbs Project had made all the difference in the world!"

How grateful to God I am for showing me what Steve needed—at just the right time.

Since suggesting The Proverbs Project to Steve, I have recommended it to many others over the years. This exercise is usually not a cure-all, not a quick fix, but it provides a powerful motivation to cooperate with God. It motivates anyone who is genuinely willing to let Him change them.

The Bible says, "The one who calls you is faithful, and he will do it" (1 Thessalonians 5:24). For more than twenty-five years, I have had the privilege of seeing God "do it" as I have coached others to be all they can be in Him, knowing that the application of His Word is the secret weapon that turns our tests into living testimonies.[1]

Coaching the Coach Tip

To experience the maximum power of God, appropriately use the Word of God. If you genuinely want God's blessing, learn how to use the Bible. Hebrews 4:12 says, "The word of God is alive and active. Sharper than any double-edged sword, it penetrates even to dividing soul and spirit, joints and marrow; it judges the thoughts and attitudes of the heart."[1]

1 Adapted from: *The Answer to Anger,* Formerly titled *Keeping Your Cool... When Your Anger is Hot!* Copyright © 2009, 2013 by Hope for the Heart, Inc. Published by Harvest House Publishers Eugene, Oregon 97402 www.harvesthousepublishers.com Used by permission.

Expanding Awareness by Understanding Essence
Michael Pfau

I will give thanks to You, for I am fearfully and wonderfully made;
Wonderful are Your works, And my soul knows it very well.
Psalm 139:14 NASB

I feel marginalized by my boss and coworkers," Mary complained as we began our first coaching session. Mary was referred to me by her husband, with whom I had worked the year before. As we spoke, she mentioned that a couple of events in the months leading up to our conversation really got her attention and that she knew she needed to change.

The first event was a blow-up she had at work with a colleague. It caught her off guard that she erupted with such anger. It also caused her great concern because she desired to be seen as someone with leadership skills and influence, a persona she had been purposely attempting to build over several years. This outburst, however, had set her back significantly. Her other concern was that she had trouble sleeping and was feeling anxiety over her career and the general direction of her life.

After she expressed these concerns, she stated that her goals for coaching were to become a better and more confident communicator. She wanted to articulate her thoughts better and be seen as a leader in the eyes of her coworkers. She desired a supervisory or management role and, having more than ten years of experience in her department, felt it was due.

As part of her personal development plan, Mary joined a Toastmasters group, began reading some good Christian books, and took some company-sponsored training. However, she still found herself internally conflicted. She mentioned feeling frustrated and helpless at her situation and wondering whether she was even in the right job.

One of the questions I posed to her was this: "What shows up when you show up?" I continued, "Imagine wearing a pink light bulb on your head and when you show up in the room the environment takes on a pink hue. What changes in a room when you show up?"

As we worked around identifying Mary's essence over several coaching calls, she realized that her presence brought warmth, energy, and acceptance. As she evaluated this new awareness, she realized that these were not the traditional qualities of a leader. She also noticed that in combination with her essence, listening intently and asking questions in meetings caused a big difference. With this new awareness and her skills, she was able to guide the discussion and be seen as a leader by her peers and boss without changing who she was as a person.

In fact, here are her own words: "Michael, I wanted to tell you about my essence. My thoughts are changing about my interactions with people. I'm observing others, at work and outside, who engage with me. What I used to think was an intimate attraction from men, I'm now seeing as an attraction to my essence (warmth, energy, acceptance) and nothing more. That has helped me relax a bit with them. And a few women at work have introduced themselves to me. We talk now in the hall. One of them has stopped by my desk to talk. I've been invited to lunch a couple times now, too. It has been fun observing this knowing what I know. Quite interesting! Thanks for introducing essence to me!"

Coaching the Coach Tip

When a client who is in conflict, internally or externally, comes for coaching consider asking them about their essence. Most people are unaware of what shows up along with them and how others see them. As in Mary's case, her lack of awareness skewed how she perceived others' responses toward her. That caused her anxiety, stress, and even anger. Those feelings led her to behave in ways that were counter to her goals. By not recognizing and being comfortable with their essence, clients often attempt to live using behaviors that aren't really authentic for them. In short, they try to be someone they weren't intended to be.

We see this same principle in 1 Samuel 17 when David came to the battlefield to deliver food to his brothers. When he heard Goliath's boasting, he decided to step up and take on the challenge to defend God's name and be Israel's champion. In his attempt to be helpful, Saul gave David his armor to wear on the battlefield. But after David tried on the armor, he discovered it just didn't fit him. David, at this point in his life, was a shepherd—not a warrior. He was not meant to use nor be weighed down by a sword, shield, and armor. For this battle he needed to use his customary sling and stones. By staying authentic to himself and obeying God, David surprised Goliath and won a great victory.

Learning From Assessments
Pam Taylor

*What we believe influences who we are and that in
turn impacts everything we do.*
Gary R. Collins

I was a brand new coach, and Jane* found me on the Internet. It felt
like it was meant to be—a match made in heaven. Woo-hoo. My
marketing is working. I dreamed of all the other clients who would
find me. Piece of cake. Just create an Internet presence and wait for
the clients to flood my calendar.

Jane and I had a great inquiry call. I heard her heart, and I
loved what I heard. She was going to be a cinch to coach. I sent out
the welcome packet, and we had the first month of appointments
set. All is well, I thought. This is working out exactly as it is supposed
to. A textbook illustration in the making.

It was, however, the beginning of one of my worst
nightmares. I understood her, but I couldn't coach her. What was
I doing wrong? It all started so well, but now she seemed "closed"
and unable to trust me. She was always late for appointments, or she
just plain forgot them. She seldom filled out a prep form. Whenever
I checked in to clarify that she wanted to work together, she said she
wanted to continue coaching. I was frustrated, but I needed her. I was
just getting started in my business, and I believed that I had to keep
whatever client God sent me. I figured I must be doing something
wrong. I would just try harder.

Before each of our scheduled calls, I skimmed my coach-
training books for clues on how to help her move forward, how to
bring out the best in her. I looked for techniques to use. I bought
a book full of powerful questions for every circumstance. I didn't
want to fail my client. If I studied harder, prayed harder, and thought

harder, certainly I could come up with a plan that would encourage her to be on time and to send the prep form and be a good client by moving forward with her life. I must have asked myself fifty times, What am I doing wrong?

It's funny, now, looking back. Jane was just acting like herself, her God-chosen self. And I was acting like my God-chosen self.

During this time, Gary Wood at Christian Coaches Network (CCN) offered a special training by Ministry Insights. Rodney Cox was going to teach us how to do the consultations for Leading from Your Strengths (LFYS), a biblically based personality assessment. I signed up. I thought it would be one more tool for my toolbox (as we say in the coaching world).

Little did I know what a life-changer the assessment would be for me. When I began to understand my own God-given, God-chosen personality, I became a better coach. I began to stop fighting my weaknesses and to embrace who God had created me to be. I began to see my strengths as strengths. And I stopped trying so hard.

Finally, I understood why Jane was not moving forward. I had been standing in her way because I had not understood myself.

It made sense to go to the next level: What if Jane took the assessment and realized how God has designed her? Wouldn't that be the affirmation she was searching for?

She did and it was. What a blessing. She began to flourish as she embraced who God created her to be. Her relationships improved and she began to accomplish things she never thought she could do.

We have been coaching together for more than two years, and she is now one of my very favorite clients. When we began together, I never would have thought that would be possible.

Coaching the Coach Tip

Bestselling author Daniel H. Pink said, "It's the coach's job to help people clarify, to see through stuff, and help them become who they really are."[1]

The key is making the choice to embrace who we really are as coaches and understanding that each person is different by the design of our Creator. We can choose to value our differences and the differences of our clients.

The Leading from Your Strengths assessment not only has been a life-changer for me but also for my clients. It helps us better understand others and ourselves. That's why I now encourage all my clients to take the LFYS assessment at the beginning of our coaching relationship. We have a consultation or two specifically around the profile results and then refer to it often in our coaching calls until it becomes second nature for them to think in that Spirit-directed awareness of self and others.

* Names and identifying details were changed to protect the client's identity.

---

[1] Daniel H. Pink quoted in Gary R Collins, *Christian Coaching* (Colorado Springs, CO, NAVPRESS, 2001), 52.

Success Does Not Make You Successful
Dr. Mark Crear

*For what shall it profit a man, if he shall gain
the whole world, and lose his own soul?*
Mark 8:36 KJV

My client Allan came to me at age forty. He was miserable, yet he appeared to be a successful CPA with a major accounting firm. In fact, most people viewed him as successful because he was making a lot of money. But Allan didn't feel successful because money wasn't as important to him as he once thought it was.

He listed his woes for me. He didn't like his boss, who showed him no respect and wouldn't look him in the face when they talked. He didn't have a romantic relationship, and he wished he did. He didn't know what he wanted to do with his life, but he knew he didn't want to be a CPA and do tax work the rest of his days.

When I asked about his values, he wasn't clear about them either. He was firm in his beliefs of God and love, but he didn't love himself. His first wife had been emotionally abusive to him, and he was hurt and afraid to recommit in any potential relationships.

Quieting the Critical Voice

At first, Allan was very reserved. He is highly intelligent and smart and as a result had a very smart gremlin-like ego that kept him stuck. I worked to help him quiet that critical voice. Eventually, he started to trust himself and me and opened up.

As I coached him to stop being so hard on himself, he began to understand that he was a good man and that he didn't have to stay forever in a job he hated. The problem was he didn't know what he wanted to do. We kept working on clearing out all the self-critical voices that stopped him from exploring other options.

During tax season he was under incredible stress. The firm was short-staffed, so he worked seven days a week with no breaks. Sometimes he would call me on the phone and just cry. I remember asking him repeatedly if he could last until April 15. He took it one day at a time, sometimes one hour at a time.

Seeing God's Intervention

Then, the most amazing thing occurred. In the middle of the tax season chaos, he called and told me what he was supposed to do with the rest of his life. He was going to quit his job and get a master's degree in education.

He made it through tax season and applied and got accepted to a great school. He quit his CPA job, moved to a new city, shared a condo with a friend, and got a part-time job making $80,000 a year.

Feeling the Love of God

Allan loves his new life. He has renewed his relationship with God and is once again seeking God's guidance in all areas of his life. He's doing brilliantly at school and definitely made the right choice to trust himself and God. While he doesn't have a serious romantic relationship, he is dating and just sent the woman he is dating to start coaching with me. So, together, I am walking them through their map of life. With Christ as the GPS, he and his girlfriend are on course to true fulfillment and joy.

Once I helped Allan to stop beating himself up emotionally, he became clear about his values and was able to trust the Divine guidance he was receiving. His life totally changed. More importantly, Allan feels like a success.

Although he is making less money, that is not the most important thing to him. He is now living according to and pursuing his top values, and that has made all the difference. Once Allan reconnected with God and sought His direction in his life, he was able to take that leap of faith and start the journey toward true happiness and success.

Coaching the Coach Tip

Success does not automatically make you feel successful. It's not uncommon to fall into societal success traps and forget about spiritual success and fulfillment. Only when we find our personal meaning of success through Christ will we feel successful.

Worldly achievement and success is not wrong. God Himself is the ultimate Achiever, starting with one of His most well known accomplishments, creation. And we want to be like Him, right? We want our sales calls to lead to big orders. We want our company's strategy to generate record-breaking profits. We want to publish our writing, sell our paintings, and to see our blogs catch on like wildfire and be appreciated by many. Why else do we start anything, other than with an intention of making it successful?

If we stop seeking God's guidance and council and start making decisions outside our core values, then we will run into that feeling of discontent just as Allan did. As Christians, we must continue to renew our minds and confirm our steps with the Lord.

"You were taught, with regard to your former way of life, to put off your old self, which is being corrupted by its deceitful desires; to be made new in the attitude of your minds; and to put on the new self, created to be like God in true righteousness and holiness" (Ephesians 4:22-24).

Picture two hands. In the right hand is the offer of true contentment, the ability to handle life's problems without being overcome by them, amazing peace that sees us through all circumstances, wisdom to know what to do, knowledge and constant direction for life, love for others, acceptance of ourselves, joy no matter what, and an eternity with God. The other hand holds all the money and power and success the world has to offer, but without any of what the right hand holds.

Which would you choose? Which would your clients choose? The Bible says, "For where your treasure is, there your heart will be also" (Matthew 6:21).

Chapter 8

Helping Clients Implement Change

To grow, clients must change. But positioning clients for successful change can be difficult. Most of us want instance success. We want big changes, so who wants to start small? In this chapter you will read how starting small can be a big help, how challenging clients to clarify their perspectives can help them catch a fresh vision, and how uncovering hidden and self-sabotaging thoughts can be valuable in break-through change. Instilling a sense of gratitude can be transforming as well. Amid the brokenness that your clients may be dealing with, remember that God is the creator of all that is good and beautiful. Hope and beauty are necessary for growth to occur.

Embrace a Small Beginning
Kevin W. McCarthy

Do not despise these small beginnings, for the Lord rejoices to see the work begin, to see the plumb line in Zerubbabel's hand.
Zechariah 4:10 NLT

It was 1994. Jorge looked me straight in the eye and matter-of-factly confessed, "Kevin, with all due respect to the amazing work we've all done, I can't lead my team to live into it."

The "amazing work" was a major strategic initiative designed to double the hospital foundation's annual fundraising capacity from $4 million to $8 million in two years. Months of planning, strategy sessions, research, thought, design, writing, and approvals went into this effort. Done right, the multiplier effect of this effort would have far-reaching impact on the overall health and services to the entire community for decades. At the patient level, research could be done, recoveries sped along, lives saved, and more. So much was at stake for so many.

As calmly as I could muster it, I asked, "What's the problem, Jorge?"

"I'm twenty pounds overweight. If I don't have the discipline to lose twenty pounds, then how can I expect my team to follow me? What kind of role model am I?"

Let's consider Jorge's professional background as the president of the hospital foundation. Working with the staff and board, we had created a succinct articulation of the organizational purpose, vision, mission, and values. A plan was in place to bring it to life. The right people were engaged. A campaign based on strategic storytelling was in development. Everything was poised for success. Yet, the real work had yet to begin. At the eleventh hour, this otherwise highly capable leader's belief system was impeding the possibilities for remarkable improvement. All the normal excuses were gone. We were left with the weight of Jorge's "truth" and the need to just begin.

Change can become a very complex and complicated matter. As coaches, however, we have a vantage point and a healthy measure of emotional distance from the seemingly irrational, yet real, perspective of the client. For Jorge, his weight was a visual metaphor and reminder of what was "wrong" with him. Most people wouldn't give their extra twenty pounds a second thought with regards to their work, but Jorge did, and that's all that mattered.

On the front end of any change, small or large, personal or professional, it always appears more monumental to the person making the transformation than the person observing or coaching it. Brainstorming and dreaming about "what it will be like when" can be intoxicatingly addictive. But at some point, the planning must end and plumb line pulled out to begin the work. That's the real work—making it happen.

Yeah, But

As a coach, how many times have you heard a client utter, "Yeah, but…"? Avoidance by conversation and planning enables us to postpone the reality of our needed transformation. Talking about making a change may feel like change, but it is incomplete without action.

Zerubbabel's challenge was to rebuild the temple. His charge required leveling a mountain and transforming its stone into a mighty place of worship. In the book of Zechariah, we read of Zerubbabel's simple act of holding the plumb line to begin the work. And God rejoices. The plumb line sets the cornerstone in the right vertical relationship so the true work can begin.

Whether rebuilding a temple, expanding the capacity of a hospital foundation, losing twenty pounds, or facing a growth opportunity, Scripture informs us, "Do not despise these small beginnings, for the Lord rejoices to see the work begin." Hint: Get started!

At some point, the true work must begin in humble earnestness. In Genesis 2:15, before the fall, the Bible says, "The

Lord God took the man and put him in the Garden of Eden to work it and take care of it." Work is God's instrument of transformation designed into His creation. How easy it is to plan and talk about what it's going to be like when...but the work must begin.

Jorge did lose his twenty pounds and gained his form. Within a year, the hospital foundation blew past its two-year goal and raised more than $12 million. Today, the only weight Jorge carries is that of being a leader of excellence.

Every Three Hours

In the spring of 2008, I faced a growing battle with being overweight. Despite my active and athletic nature, my years of unhealthy eating and misconceptions had packed on the pounds. Over the top of my athletic body, I wore my fat suit. One day I planned to take it off. One day....

A health coaching company booked me sight unseen to be their national convention keynote speaker. In three months, the pioneer of the On-Purpose® Approach to life and work would stand before 850 health coaches as a fat guy. More importantly, I was not a good, honest steward of the temple God had provided me. What was my On-Purpose message all about really?

Something had to change. Lori became my health coach. She asked me a simple, yet defining question: "Kevin, can you eat every three hours?" Of course, I could. In essence, she set the plumb line and the work began with a small beginning.

On stage three months later and fifty pounds lighter, I was in the company of passionate life-changing coaches. More than my weight had changed. Yes, I lost weight, but more importantly, I gained health, clarity of thought, confidence, and a return to being a good steward of the person made in God's image.

Clients and friends asked me what I did. I referred my wife and eight others to my health coach. Judith lost those pesky mid-section twenty pounds that sneak up a pound or two per year. My friends came off medications, cleared their minds, and rediscovered life beyond the fog of being fat.

136

How could we keep this gift of good health to ourselves? With Lori's mentorship, late in 2008 Judith and I launched a health coaching business. Since then, more than two thousand clients have returned to good health in three-hour increments. Truly. We live by the phrase "Do not despise these small beginnings" as we rebuild the temple of the body.

When looking up at your insurmountable mountain of change, get with your coach to plan and prepare.

- Your purpose ignites you with a reason why.
- Your vision inspires you to see what can be.
- Your mission charts the path.
- Your values govern your decisions.

Your on-purpose plan is solid. Now, get to work.

Coaching the Coach Tip

Embrace the small start by identifying what's next; keep it simple, reasonable, and measurable. Pray, begin, complete it, and repeat. Once you've accomplished your change, share your lessons learned.

Time for a New Vision
Anne Denmark

Brethren, I do not regard myself as having laid hold of it yet; but one thing I do: forgetting what lies behind and reaching forward to what lies ahead, I press on toward the goal for the prize of the upward call of God in Christ Jesus.
Philippians 3:13-14 NASB

Maggie is an amazing woman. Her insatiable passion to grow in her faith matches her transparency. Her no-nonsense approach is refreshing. I am sure we all dream of having our days filled with coaching clients just like her.

Maggie came to Christ shortly before we started coaching. She was in serious debt and really feared that someday she would end up living out of a cardboard box. Her pastor prayed that God would accelerate her spiritual growth, and his wife encouraged Maggie to work with me.

Maggie wanted radical change in all areas of her life. "I feel like I want to blow open all the doors to my life and shine some light on them." She wanted freedom from past addictions, bad men, and fast cars. She wanted the abundant life Jesus came to give her.

As part of this abundant life, she also wanted to get out of the bondage of debt. Her battle cry was, "Let's do this thing." So God, Maggie, and I formed a coaching partnership to adjust attitudes, break old habits, and dispel lies. And in her words, she "worked her butt off" for several years until finally she found herself writing the following in her prep form:

Sooo many challenges—let's dive right in:

It has been an identity crisis to be almost debt free. I started having panic attacks. Went to doc—thought I was having a heart attack. He almost laughed. Basically said: I have the heart of a 20-year-old. There is nothing in my brain on being debt free. Nothing. It's a big blank slate. I'm growing more accustomed to it daily but honestly I'm checking my bank account twice a day just to make sure I'm not dreaming this up.

My heart has changed. I do not want to go and spend. This has been a lifelong obsession. Got money—go spend. Now I can't wait to get paid to pay something off!

I prepared for my call with Maggie by clearing my desk, pulling her file, and re-reading the words I had highlighted on her prep form. "It has been an identity crisis to be almost debt free."

So what is this all about? I wondered. Here was Maggie almost at the finish line of achieving a goal she'd wanted for some time. Now instead of jubilation and joy she is feeling a sense of crisis and panic. I asked myself, What made finally achieving her goals so scary?

The phone rang then and I answered: "Hi, Maggie, it is good to hear your voice." I checked her mood and frame of mind by asking, "How do you come to our call today?"

"I am weary and don't feel much passion. I am doubting myself these days."

That day I was especially thankful that our coaching calls always began with a fresh breath of Scripture followed by prayer. Maggie and I acknowledged God's presence, asked for His direction, and promised to give Him the glory for the fruit of our coaching. By the time we finished praising Him for her wins and insights, I could hear the vigor in Maggie's voice beginning to return. Then, at her request we dove into the topic at hand, her debt-free identify crisis.

As I listened to her describe in detail her panicky feelings in her new, almost-debt-free status something was not adding up. I recalled her words on the prep form, "Now I can't wait to get paid to pay something off."

I thought, What will you do with the money now? I also felt tension because my gut told me that Maggie was at a turning point that needed exploring. But how? Suddenly I remembered the coaching technique of drawing out clear distinctions. The thought came so fast and unconsciously that I knew God was in this moment.

I'd learned that distinctions highlight the difference between two things that are incongruent. They bring greater clarity and are a wonderful tool for discovery.

So I asked several questions highlighting distinctions: "What is the difference between 'getting away from something like debt' and 'being called to do something with the money you save'?; What is the difference between 'struggling to survive' and 'living on purpose'?"

We continued to explore distinctions until finally she exclaimed, "That's it. I need a fresh vision."

Working through these distinctions had given Maggie a new perspective. She continued, "I have been struggling so hard to survive that I don't know what's next."

"What would you like to be able to do with your money?" I asked. Passion filled her voice as she said, "I want to save up enough money so that I can take off work for several months a year and serve with the Convoy of Hope."

As she began to articulate what God had already placed on her heart, it reminded me of Paul's words to the saints in Ephesus: "For we are His workmanship, created in Christ Jesus for good works, which God prepared beforehand so that we would walk in them" (Ephesians 2:10 NASB).

By the time Maggie said goodbye that day her mind was no longer a blank slate. She had a new vision filled with thoughts by God. We were both aware that we had participated in a life-changing session.

Coaching the Coach Tip

Let me be quick to say that not all coaching calls result in a dramatic insight like this one. It occurred after working together for several years. Maggie had learned to trust me and had an amazing desire to grow. Most of the time she kept moving steadily forward one-step at a time.

The transforming power of this call came from God, the ultimate Life Coach. He makes all the difference. Coaches don't have to have all the answers, but as Christian coaches you and I can relax knowing God does. We have the intimacy of our Creator walking beside us and working through us. If you have not yet experienced this kind of moment in your coaching, I encourage you to catch a fresh vision of God's call on your life. Be aware of His presence when you are working with your clients. Listen for His voice and move on His promptings. That's what makes you a distinctly Christian coach.

Wait Until Dark
June Hunt

When I am afraid, I will put my trust in You.
Psalm 56:3 NASB

Over the years, Ellen and I had enjoyed a warm, productive coaching relationship in which I'd had the opportunity to help her with a variety of issues from dating to achieving greater career success. A mature Christian leader with years of Bible training, Ellen was transparent, bright, and motivated to grow and learn. Not only did she work full-time at a Christian counseling ministry, she also led recovery groups at her church and was a sought-after women's mentor.

But one day, as I was chatting with Ellen about an invitation I'd received to write and teach on the topic of fear, I noticed her demeanor become increasingly dim. Her downcast eyes suggested something was sapping her soul.

After a lengthy silence, Ellen looked up and said quietly, "I've never told anyone this, June, and it's so crazy I can hardly believe it, myself—I mean, I'm fifty-three years old—but I'm afraid of the dark."

"Oh, Ellen," I said. "How difficult that must be. I feel honored that you would trust me with something so deeply personal. I'd love to know more if you'd care to share."

"Each time I enter a dark room, I'm stricken with fear," she began. "I imagine something jumping out and grabbing me. It happens every time I walk into my apartment at night, into my garage, or even into my own bathroom. I can't begin to tell you how many times I've prayed and asked God to remove the fear, but it's still there. It's embarrassing to admit I'm struggling with something so irrational."

As I gently probed, I learned that Ellen, the youngest of four, had been forced as a child by her siblings to enter a dark room in search of her "kidnapped" doll. Ellen's brother and sisters would string the doll in the middle of the room, using yards of invisible thread. If she wanted her doll back, six-year-old Ellen had to venture into the dark room, alone. After a few steps, she'd become entangled like a fly snagged in a spider's web. Panicked, she'd thrash and lunge, grasping in the dark for her beloved doll. By the time she'd retrieve Thumbelina, Ellen was tearful and terrified.

Flash forward fifty years. It was clear that Ellen genuinely desired to walk in faith, not in fear. To do so, however, she needed to understand that, like beauty, fear is in the mind of the beholder. Ellen needed to conquer her thinking before she could quell her fears.

"Ellen," I asked, "does God's Word tell us fear is wrong?"

"I think so."

"Actually, God never assumes we will live without fear. In fact, His Word specifically addresses fear by telling us, 'When I am afraid, I will put my trust in You' (Psalm 56:3 NASB). Notice, this verse doesn't say, 'if,' but, 'when'—'When I am afraid….' It's undeniable. At times, both you and I will have fear. However, we don't have to be consumed by fear."

"But how can I help but be consumed when I'm so afraid? It's not a conscious decision, June. It just takes over."

"In reality you have the power to take over. When you take charge of your mind, you'll take control of your fear, instead of allowing fear to take control of you. So, when you find yourself in fear-producing situations, would you be willing to try a new strategy?"

"Sure. Anything that would help."

"Okay, then, here's what I recommend: Each time you enter a dark room and feel that sense of panic and dread, I want you to say Psalm 56:3 out loud. 'When I am afraid, I will put my trust in you.' And don't just say the words, but think about each word as you're saying it. Say it over and over, as many times as you need to until you feel your peace returning. I want you to tell your fears the Word of God. Does that sound doable?"

"I'll try it, starting tonight!"

"Great. And let's talk next week. I'd like to know how it goes."

As Ellen left, I found myself wondering how, given all of the in-depth coaching over the last year, I'd failed to address an area that was causing her so much angst. I realized I'd assumed that Ellen, being so naturally forthcoming, would have brought up the issue long before now. But she hadn't. And I hadn't asked. I never asked if there were secret places where she still found herself stuck.

About ten days after our initial conversation, Ellen and I spoke by phone. What a thrill to hear her ebullient progress report.

"I can't even say, for sure, when it began to happen—or how—but, little by little, June, I'm seeing my fear of the dark fade away. I've been saying Psalm 56:3 every single time I find fear welling up inside me. At first, I felt a little silly, talking aloud in my apartment entryway. Sometimes, I repeat the verse six or seven times, just walking around the apartment turning on the lights. But, honestly, it's amazing how saying aloud that one simple Scripture has had such an impact. I'm finding that I'm needing to say it less and less because, finally, after all those years, the fear is losing its grip."

Over the next few months, I checked back with Ellen and learned that her fear of the dark had vanished almost completely. And, from time to time, when it did try to make a comeback, she'd fight back with Psalm 56:3.

Ellen's update explains why I love lifting up God's Word to others. It also explains an important coaching lesson: By taking the initiative to gently draw out any dark secret, anything self-sabotaging, we present a priceless gift to those we seek to help.

Coaching the Coach Tip

Even if you coach clients you know well, even those mature and grounded in the Bible, don't assume they have no hidden areas holding them back. Take the initiative to ask, "Is there any area where you feel stuck—something you can't seem to overcome?" Then listen patiently and actively to their heart's reply.

Listen and Trust
Dr. John Rottschafer

Take note of this: Everyone should be quick to listen, slow to speak
James 1:19

I first met Kim after the tragic death of her fiancé. She was hurt, disillusioned, and confused about God's plan for her life. During the course of our coaching, she came to peace with her loss and acknowledged the beginning stages of a new relationship with a man several years her senior. Eventually, this relationship grew into a marriage full of hope and promise—or so it seemed at the start.

Over the next decade, Kim returned three more times for coaching. Each time, she was unhappy with her marriage relationship. Her husband seemed dissatisfied with her. Recognizing the power of her role as wife, she clearly stated, "I want to learn how to be a better wife." She hoped that by being a better wife, she would please her husband and their relationship would improve.

After each round of coaching, Kim embraced her marriage with new commitment and vigor. Clearly, her marriage was very important to her, as were the vows she had made. Bolstered by her Christian values and belief system, she reported that she was in this relationship "for the long haul."

Personally, I was impressed by the dedication and resolve Kim displayed. Though she had a tendency to slump into despair, she knew what she wanted and was willing to work for it, by herself and with her husband. Her respect for marriage felt comfortable to me, as did her desire to take action and grow. Our coaching sessions honored her goals, but also affirmed what I held dear.

Years passed between seasons of coaching, yet each time the coaching theme remained the same: improve the marriage. Then, after twelve years of marriage, Kim asked to meet again. "I need you

145

to help me leave my marriage." Immediately, my mind went to the need to reconnect her with her values. Obviously, I thought, she had drifted from them and lost contact with what was most important to her. But she said, "If I don't leave, I'll die—if not physically, then emotionally."

Her focus and resolve were familiar, but her direction had changed. She expressed the same Christian values but brought with them a new sense of reality and truth. This was not a passive giving-in to the easy road, but rather a reallocation of her resources. She had turned a corner. As she said, "There is no turning back. I just want to stay as healthy as possible during this process. I want to do it right."

It became apparent that I needed to shift my focus to keep in step with Kim. With her change in goal came a corresponding need for me to reassess and refocus my commitment to Kim and to her new goal. I needed to value her more than the marriage she needed to leave. I needed to listen, learn, and trust that God was loving and guiding her as she walked her new path.

After several months, Kim successfully emerged from an emotionally abusive marriage that was rife with domination, manipulation, accusation, and isolation. While frequently challenged during these months, she also clearly developed strength, awareness, and discernment previously unknown to her. As a result, Kim still values marriage and hopes to experience it someday in a deeper, more God-glorifying way as the new person she has become.

The path of divorce Kim chose has long been a path that we in the Christian church have struggled with. Yet, it was vital for me, as her coach, to recognize and embrace the fact that God can use even a path of brokenness to grow His children and bring glory to His name.

Today, Kim reports a new joy in living. She also celebrates the simple freedom once again to breathe.

Coaching the Coach Tip

As we work with our clients, it is important to ensure that the goals of our coaching are the client's goals, not simply our goals. To do this, we must listen closely to them and not assume that we know what their goal is or should be. We need to trust what we hear and resist the temptation to manipulate the stated goals to better fit our "wisdom."

While at times it may seem shortsighted to follow the client's lead, it clearly is not. Rather, it is profoundly respectful, both of the client's wisdom and right to choose. Kim went through three rounds of coaching to be a better wife before she was ready to see her marriage as the dangerous, abusive relationship it was. Had I suggested that perspective to her from the start, she likely would have rejected the idea as assumptive, insulting, and unkind. And she would have been right. Also, in doing so, I would have jeopardized the coaching process needed to strengthen and empower her so she could see the truth on her own.

Listen. Be patient. Trust the process. God is at work. Good things will come.

Gratitude, the Healing Attitude
Linda Knasel

Submit to God and be at peace with him;
in this way prosperity will come to you.
Job 22:21

My clients have a lot of stress and anxiety, and I'm learning that attitude plays a huge role in these emotions. I believe attitudes are dramatically impacted by America's culture. We are a society driven to achieve, keep up with the Joneses, and acquire bigger and better things. Many kids today come from two-income households and have more material possessions than previous generations. People are overextending their personal resources yet are still driven to achieve more. They think they want more for themselves and their children, but they aren't exactly sure why.

History has proven that increased prosperity does not always equal increased satisfaction. As my clients are caught up in the cycle of materialism, they find themselves dealing with insurmountable relationship conflict, anguish, hurt, and bitterness. Most of the time they don't realize this is caused by their underlying mindset or attitude. Scripture has a term for this; it's called "covetousness."

If I suspect covetousness is the source of my clients' stress and anxiety, I stop and ask myself the following questions: Why is he pursuing what he wants? Is she headed in the right direction? What's his attitude toward achieving his desired goal? Are her attitudes healthy and productive, or destructive?

If a client is seeking to grow based on a selfish desire, greed, or materialism, then I don't believe it's in their best interest that I coach him or her to achieve more.

For instance, Adriana came to me and was upset because she wasn't as popular as some of her friends. She had just spent more than $300 buying bathing suits to look cute on the beach and gain attention from the guys and be popular. She'd incurred major bills for highlights, make-up, lotions, clothes, and the latest shoes and bags.

As a coach and licensed counselor, when a deep-seeded issue like covetousness is revealed, I have to decide whether I can move my client forward using coaching or counseling. Sometimes coaching is all that's needed, while other times counseling practices are necessary to help a client resolve underlying difficulties.

When I decide to continue coaching the client who is dealing with materialism, I found success in helping him or her focus on gratefulness and contentment. When clients become grateful and content with God and His provisions, they become more peaceful and less anxious. Clients who are able to replace stress with gratitude end up being less self-absorbed and prideful, and more thankful for those around them. Appreciative clients make better choices and enjoy more positive relationships.

In Adriana's case, she began to learn to thank God for the things she had and how to recognize Him as the giver of these gifts. We worked on how to show gratefulness and how the lifestyle she was living was robbing her of the true joy of fellowship with God and the friendships that God placed in her life. We worked on developing some time for her to rest and count her blessings and reduced the time-robbers that were holding her back from true joy. We discussed what her material choices were bringing her and what she really wanted. We then set goals that would really move her in a direction that would bring her success based on solid biblical principles.

Coaching the Coach Tip

How do we coach to help our clients feel grateful to God? One technique I've used is a thirty-one-day gratitude journal. On the left-hand side of an open journal, I ask my clients to list the three big stresses that impact each day. Then I ask them to pray and give these situations to God, followed by reading a chapter from the book of Proverbs that matches the day of the month. While reading from Proverbs, clients look for God's wisdom that addresses one of the three stressful situations and then apply the principles that come to light. That evening, on the opposite side of the open journal, they list the blessings they've noticed throughout the day. Depending on the circumstances, they normally do this for a total of thirty-one days.

The gratitude journal exercise helps my clients focus on the fine and good things God has to offer rather than the stresses in life. In addition, it allows the Spirit of God to move their mindsets from worry, grumbling, murmuring, and complaining to seeing blessings and being grateful.

Once my clients have a chance to focus on what they are grateful for, I can help them problem-solve the real issues that are nagging them. After seeing how much God loves and cares for them, they gain a proper perspective and focus.

The gratitude journal is one way coaches can help their clients reduce stress caused by misguided desires. As my clients seek God and trust Him for insights, they are driven more by God and less by the pressures of society. I've been amazed witnessing how God uses a simple journal to change the attitudes of my clients and bring contentment into their lives.

Why Beauty Matters for Balance Against Brokenness
Dr. Catherine Hart Weber

The Christian coaching relationship holds out the hope and message of God's beauty through love, goodness, and redemption as His divine antidote to the discouragement and brokenness in and around us.
Dr. Catherine Hart Weber

Beauty and hope are essential for growth. The essence of my program for coaches—Flourish in Life and Relationships Coaching—is captured by the profound story of a woman who admired pottery. At a recent art show, she came across a large bowl that particularly caught her eye.

The bowl had an amazingly wavy shape, and its beauty captured her heart. It was a symbolic gift from the sea to her. It was as if this full, foaming, rolling wave was calling to her, offering treasures and messages. Deep calling to deep.

The sunlight glistened off the glossy tranquil ocean tones finish, reflecting the full spectrum of colors. It was a reminder to her to be present in the now, living fully alive in every moment.

She was compelled to touch the invitingly smooth surface. Her fingers ran gently over the waves, falling into the safety of the full, round bowl.

Only skilled hands of the potter and the high heat of the fiery furnace could produce such smoothness, such beauty.

It was a metaphor for her journey. All her senses were awakened to expressing and giving form to what her heart and soul was experiencing.

The bowl was a thing of beauty and inspired images she wanted to continue to embrace. She had to take it home with her.

Unfortunately, the bowl was expensive—too expensive for her to purchase. So she moved along. She tried focusing on another potter's three small pots that were fused together, symbolic of a three-fold cord, unbroken.

The next day, however, she just couldn't get the beauty of the wave bowl off her mind. She had to go back and admire it once more. Maybe the artist would be willing to give her a discount. She had saved some Christmas money for such a time as this.

The potter was flattered by her admiration of his work. They had a great conversation. As she turned to ask him about the beautiful wave bowl, her bag knocked over a large vase behind her. It fell to the ground, shattering in dozens of small pieces.

She stared at her feet and the broken pieces that surrounded her. She was in shock. How could this happen? She had come to pursue and acquire beauty, and now she was faced with brokenness—very expensive brokenness. Right then and there something inside her also shattered. She broke down, sobbing audibly. Yes, she felt badly about the loss of the art. Yes, she understood she'd have to pay for the expensive vase and she'd have nothing to show for having done so. But her tears were about something more, something much deeper.

The Balance of Beauty

You see, most of her life had been spent dealing with or paying for brokenness. She had lived with cancer for more than twenty years. During the past twelve years, it had been her consistent companion. She was on her fifth round of chemo, and her treatment cost was in the thousands of dollars. Her life revolved around the damaging consequences of her broken body and other shattered things around her.

She just couldn't deal with one more broken thing. She couldn't just pay for more brokenness and walk away with no hope or beauty.

The potter offered to let her pay wholesale for both the broken vase and the wave bowl. Through the artist's generosity, the Spirit of God gave the woman an inner gift. She was released from

152

disappointment, discouragement, and brokenness, so she could keep embracing hope and pursuing beauty. She left with a bag of shattered vase pieces and the beautiful wave bowl—the balance of beauty against the brokenness.

Coaching the Coach Tip

Humans are hardwired to desire to grow, to love, to pursue what matters—love, hope, and beauty. As a Christian coach, we have the privilege to journey alongside others, helping them find the balance between brokenness and growing in love, hope, and beauty.

Many of those we coach struggle with doubts, disappointments, and discouragement. There is a tendency to teeter on the edge of freedom and fear, doubt and hope. Dealing only with broken pieces and disappointment keeps us deprived, holds us back. We tell ourselves, beauty is too extravagant. I can't justify it. These hopes and goals are too unrealistic, unreachable. I can't enjoy beauty and imagine reaching my dreams because I'm too afraid. I've got to clean up all my failures and broken things before I invest in anything of beauty.

What many of us don't realize is that Jesus' love and beauty set us free. From the moment we invite Him into our life, He brings light into our darkness. He makes beauty from ashes. He provides ultimate peace and hope through His Spirit so we can flourish now. The coaching relationship guides others to open their eyes and hearts to see all that Christ is, what He provides, and what He promises to do—give us hope, goodness, and beauty.

Encourage clients to imagine what this vibrant life, living fully alive in God, looks like for them. Assure them that pursuing hope and the beauty of Christ's transforming life in them matters.

It is a journey. It is a lifestyle. They are partnering with the Spirit to have the mind of Christ, creating practical daily rhythms, identifying priorities, and setting goals.

We can't escape this life's pain, darkness, and brokenness. We all have doubts, disappointments, and discouragement. But we can open our lives and help our clients open their lives to the Holy Spirit. We can help them hold on to their hopes, dreams, and visions from God—His love, joy, peace, hope—and beauty.

As a hope-giver, we guide others in anticipating, embracing, and living out the vision of God's hope, love, and beauty, creatively exploring ways to live fully alive, right where we are, amidst life's brokenness.

Chapter 9

Adjusting Your Strategies

As coaches, we consistently have to be willing to evaluate and reevaluate our style and approach with clients. Sometimes we focus too much on impressing our clients rather than considering what is best for them. At other times, we may have confidence in our abilities rather than seeking the wisdom of God through prayer. You might be so focused on holding your clients accountable to action steps that you overlook some key relational issues they are struggling with. Or perhaps you catch yourself attempting to lead a client down a path you think he should take, or you struggle with the question of referring your client to another coach or counselor.

As a coach, be willing to adjust and readjust your strategies and intentionally choose to do what is best for your client.

Is My Goal to Impress or Bless?
Georgia Shaffer

Do nothing out of selfish ambition or vain conceit. Rather,
in humility value others above yourselves, not looking to your
own interests but each of you to the interests of the others.
Philippians 2:3-4

Georgia," my client Amy, who is a life coach, had written, "I'm hoping during our session tomorrow you can help me with two difficult clients. I'm not sure how to handle them."

I was reviewing the pre-session form I ask my clients to complete and return before each appointment. It helps me get an idea of what has happened in their lives since our last appointment. I include questions such as "What has been on my mind the most since my last session?" "What has been my biggest joy or victory, and how does it link to my stated goals?" and "What would I like to focus on during this session?"

My immediate reaction upon reading Amy's request for help with two difficult clients was to pray, "Lord, help me be brilliant. Help me not to look stupid but to find a solution." I cringed. "Okay, Lord, give me wisdom."

A few days earlier, I had listened to an interview with Christian counselor and author Larry Crabb. At one point, he said to the interviewer, "I am always trying to pay attention to where my heart is. Am I trying to bless my client or impress him or her?"

As a coach, I'm all too aware that unless I pay attention, my natural tendency is to want to impress my clients or to solve their problems for them, neither of which is my role as a coach. For me, it's important to pray before my coaching sessions and also during our time together, asking God to guide me by His Holy Spirit.

Before Amy's particular session when she asked for help with her two difficult clients, I strongly felt God leading me to listen and then pray with her. So after she described each client, I suggested we pray. I knew that was not what she wanted, but I was obedient to what I believed God was prompting me to do.

"You know what?" Amy said when I finished. "As you were praying, I just realized a key comment my one client made in our initial session. I had totally forgotten about it, but now everything is falling into place. I have a much better understanding about what is going on with her."

Sure enough, a few days later, Amy emailed me to say that her client had experienced a major breakthrough. As a coach, Amy was thrilled to be part of God's powerful miracle in this person's life. And I was in awe of God's ability to use Amy and me in the lives of those we coach.

At our next session, Amy and I discussed this particular client. I admitted to her that my initial response was to come up with some brilliant solution.

"It's interesting you should say that," she said, "because I wanted you to fix it for me. I wanted you to say, 'Well, this is what I would do,' but you didn't. Instead, you said, 'Let's pray and ask God for discernment,' which I had not wanted to do. I wanted you to tell me what to do."

We both laughed.

"However," Amy continued, "it was what was best for me. Your suggestion that we stop and pray really stood out to me as a much more caring thing to do. While we were praying, I remembered something pivotal that really helped that particular situation, and reaffirmed the value of taking everything to God in prayer."

This experience is a good example of the Apostle Paul's wisdom in Philippians 2:3-4, which is very applicable in our coaching practices. To paraphrase Paul, do nothing out of the desire to impress, but keep your heart centered on the goal of honoring the Lord.

Coaching the Coach Tip

You, too, might have times when you struggle to please a client. When someone is paying for your services, you don't want to disappoint him or her. Even if you have only one dissatisfied client, you understand how quickly negative comments about your coaching practice can spread by word of mouth and over the Internet.

There is no doubt that during that appointment with Amy I felt like I had copped out. I was aware that her perception was something like, "I'm paying you to listen and then you only say, 'Let's pray.'" For me, it was humbling to do what I did. It required that I take a real risk. But having the courage to obey God opened the door for Him to clearly show Amy what she needed to see.

As a Christian coach, make sure you are spending time communicating with God on a regular basis. Like Eli taught Samuel (1 Samuel 3:9), we want always to be saying, "Speak, LORD, for your servant is listening."

My quiet time in the early morning helps me to cultivate the habit of listening and checking my heart. Taking a minute or two before each session to pray enables me to recheck my motives and ask God to show me if my real desire is to honor myself or to honor Him.

Be aware. Recognize your tendency at times may be to appear insightful and skilled as a coach. There are going to be situations when you and your client will struggle with a problem or a seemingly insurmountable obstacle. I'm not saying that as a coach you never make a suggestion to your client. But if your heart's desire is to help your clients, then be willing routinely to ask yourself something similar to what Larry Crabb often asks himself. Would you say you are trying to impress or bless your clients?

Prayer: A Tool or a Lifeline?
Denise Baumann

Pray without ceasing.
1 Thessalonians 5:17 NASB

As a Christian life coach, I open each session with prayer. As a Christ-follower, I want the Holy Spirit to do His best work in the time I have with my client. This habit can easily become just a check mark on my to-do list for each session. So how do I keep prayer as my lifeline and not merely a session-opening tool?

The answer starts with my personal prayer life, which has taken on a whole new level of importance and growth in the past few years. During this time, I felt compelled to read the Gospels (Matthew, Mark, Luke, and John) four times in one year. As I read about the life of Jesus, I saw how important prayer was to Him. It was so important that He went to the desert for forty days to fast and pray as recorded in Matthew 4:1-11. He got up early in the morning and, according to Mark 1:35, went to a secluded, quiet place to be alone with His Father and pray. The disciples saw the importance Jesus placed on prayer and asked for prayer instruction in Luke 11:1. Seeing the importance Jesus placed on prayer and knowing my own spiritual neediness, I committed to being more like Him in this regard.

During this time, I had an opportunity to take part in the Cornerstone Formation Ministries training program taught by Dr. Terry Wardle. It was titled "Ministry of Formational Prayer." In this training, we were taught to pray expectantly, understanding God will answer if we give Him a chance.

The Bible is clear in James 4:2: "You do not have, because you do not ask" (ESV). Learning to pray expectantly transformed my spiritual and personal life. Since I've begun to do this, I have witnessed firsthand how God the Father communicates through prayer to one client after another on a variety of issues.

If I am in a session and I sense my client is struggling or we seem to hit a wall, I may take a minute silently to ask God for insight. I may also ask the client to ask God for an answer, and we will take a minute together in prayer, asking for an immediate answer. Many times He does. At other times, as a homework assignment, I request that clients ask God for clear direction for the next week.

These prayers can change how clients view God. I had one client change from not wanting to burden God with her problems because "He has so much to take care of already" to understanding "God does really care about my everyday life." She now asks God about every decision. She does not want to make any changes without praying first, because she has seen what prayer can do.

Coaching the Coach Tip

Because of the transformation of my personal prayer life, I now incorporate prayer in each coaching session. Wow! What a difference it has made. I no longer worry that I won't have enough tools in my tool belt to help each client in his or her specific area of need. The Holy Spirit prompts me throughout the session (because I am in constant prayer) with ideas and options. The Holy Spirit will give my client and me the answers we need if we give Him the chance. Does this mean I don't do my homework as a coach? May it never be. I still read every day and research resources. As I pray for my clients, I now ask God through prayer to show me what my clients need before I meet with them. So many times God does just that.

Balance from the Inside Out
Dr. Henry Cloud

I am the true vine, and my Father is the gardener. He
cuts off every branch in me that bears no fruit,
while every branch that does bear fruit
he prunes so that it will be even more fruitful.
John 15:1-2

I remember one time when a Fortune 500 company asked me if I wanted to come and speak on "time management" for their leaders. I immediately said, "No, not really," and told them that it was not a topic that really grabbed me.

The woman came back and said that it was very important to them and they devoted a lot of training to it, and she asked if I would reconsider.

So, I asked her, "Have you had training on time management before?"

"Why, yes," she said. "We have had a lot of emphasis on it."

"And are the same people who were productive and not overstressed before still the ones who are productive and not overstressed, and the ones who were disorganized, always overstressed, and not as productive about the same as they were before but now have a new colorful notebook binder with a bunch of time-management tools that they carry around?"

She laughed and had to agree with the reality of what their time-management seminars had gotten them.

So I made a deal with her. "I will be glad to come and speak on time management if you let me speak on the way that I think time management really works," I said.

"What do you mean?" she asked.

"In your time-management seminars, have you ever talked about the real reason Sally never finishes anything on time is that she spends a lot of the day lingering in other people's offices or by the coffee machine? And that the real reason that she does that is that she is lonely and is trying to fill that need for connection at work?" I asked.

"Uh, no...can't say that we have talked about that," she replied.

"Or have you talked about that the real reason Shawn has too much to do and can't finish it all? That it might be that his perfectionism keeps him from sending out an email or a report without checking and over-checking it so many times because he is afraid of what someone might think if it is not perfect, so he becomes a bottleneck for the whole department?" I asked.

"No, haven't talked about that either," she said.

"Or maybe that Susie is always behind because she can't tell Sally to stop interrupting her when she is working and that she doesn't have time to cover for John in still another project that he was not able to get done?" I wondered aloud.

"Okay, I get it," she said. "No, those are not the kind of discussions we have had."

"Well, I will be glad to come if I can talk about the way that time management really works, meaning that it is really about more than time. I think that most people eight or ten years old understand time. But what they struggle with is managing themselves. I would love to talk about self-management and how it affects time, productivity, and stress," I said.

"Let's do it!" she said.

We did and had a great time. Their leaders got into deeper discussions about the real reasons that their work lives were out of control. And when such discussions get to our responsibility as coaches, those reasons become very important.

In my view, coaches often come in two types. One is what I would call "structure-adding coaches." The value that they bring to clients is the structure that they cannot provide for themselves, such as mission, goals, strengths, clarification, objectives, time-lines,

162

metrics, milestones, accountability, schedules, resource allocation, and so forth. Those things are very important and are of true value to many people. I have seen businesses turn around when accountability is brought to the table to help people define a direction and keep moving down a path.

But there is more to coaching than adding structure. And that is where the second type of coach comes in. This type of coach will ask "why" when someone is unable to keep the direction, goals, and accountability that they have set for themselves. It goes deeper than a time-management manual or a goal-setting notebook.

And that "why" question always leads to two important areas for a person to examine in order to grow and get better. First, it leads to their own character issues, or issues about their own makeup. I addressed these in my book *Integrity* as a lack of integration of important personal issues or character traits needed for success, such as the "ability to maintain trust," the "ability to find and live in the truth of reality," the "ability to embrace negative reality," and a few others. These are significant intrapersonal issues that higher-level coaching must address for people to realize the full potential of their gifts, talents, and opportunities. As 2 Peter 1:8 tells us, character and fruitfulness are very much intertwined.

Second, it leads to the interpersonal issues that may be behind their inability to get to the proverbial next level, or are causing the problems they are facing. Inevitably, there are relational issues that keep people stuck or get them off track or create conflicts for them that they do not know how to resolve. Sometimes these are with bosses, sometimes with peers, and sometimes with direct reports. But the real reasons that often drive performance issues, stress, burnout, and workaholism are actually relational in nature. Good coaching asks the questions that get to the root of the issue.

Sometimes these two sets of issues show that there is a need for therapy, and a coach will refer the person for that kind of work. But often they are not of a clinical nature and coaching can help the person gain the real-life skills that provide results and growth. The difference though is that the coachee is not just filling out boxes in a time-management or goals worksheet but growing as a person instead. That is growth from the inside out, as character and relational abilities improve. And that is the coaching that brings fruits that last forever.

Coaching the Coach Tip

It is important that we remember that all balance flows from the inside out. As Jesus said, it is the tree that produces the fruit. If there are fruits such as imbalance, overwork, bad health, stress, or poor performance, you must look at the real issues inside the person that are producing those fruits. If you do, and coach them well, the outside fruit will change as well.[1]

---

1 Re-printed from *Christian Coaching Today*, Volume 1, Issue 4 with permission of the American Association of Christian Counselors.

It's about Your Client
Sandra Dopf Lee

Life is change. Growth is optional. Choose wisely.
Karen Kaiser Clark

About five years into my coaching career, I learned one of the best lessons for my clients and me as a professional coach. My confidence as a coach had really grown during those years, but I needed to be reminded not to stray from basic coaching principles.

Suzy hired me to be her divorce-life coach and help her rebuild her life after this major life transition. As with any other first session with a client, I asked her to take my Emerging Life Scan survey and questionnaire. Once she finished, we discussed the top two areas of her life that needed emergency-room-style attention. After a more in-depth question-and-answer dialogue, we both agreed to begin focusing on her finances and some concerns she had with her children.

Money or the lack thereof was a constant battle for Suzy after her divorce. She tried to stick to a budget, but she admitted that never worked because she said finances overwhelmed her. She admitted she wasn't good with money management. When I asked about her income, she defensively talked about how she couldn't work because her kids were only nine and twelve and she needed to be the stay-at-home mom that she had been during the marriage. Her sole income at that time came from child support and alimony.

During Suzy's divorce settlement negotiations, she let everyone know she wanted the marital home. That had been where she had brought both her babies as newborns, and it was the only home they knew. Because Suzy had felt so strongly about her nonnegotiable desire to keep the house, her attorney moved full-speed ahead to make sure she was awarded this possession. Now, two years following the divorce, this prized win had become the biggest financial burden in her life. The mortgage, taxes, and maintenance were draining her financially.

After discussing how Suzy was dealing with finances, we proceeded to the second life area in which she needed some coaching—parenting as a single mother.

"Give me three or four sentences to describe your life as a single mother," I said.

"I love my children very much," Suzy said. "They are the greatest blessing in my life, and I thank God for them every day. I am a very good mother, but my kids aren't doing well with the divorce. My ex-husband is a Disneyland dad who never does any homework with them. They get to go out to eat every time he has them, and he buys toys and junk they don't need. I have to be the responsible parent. Every time they come home from a visit with him, the kids are so tired and grumpy. And that just sets our week off to be out of control."

"Why does it set your whole week off this way? How does his weekend interaction control your next week?"

"Well, the kids are already tired, so they are late getting ready every morning, which makes them late for school. Then because everyone is running late and is grumpy in the mornings, we can't find anything to wear. Their stuff isn't in their book bags. When they get home in the afternoon, they want to play with friends or watch television. When I say they can't and need to get their homework done and get ready for the next day, they get so upset and tell me they have more fun when they are with their dad.

"I know my house isn't much fun, so I usually let them have a couple of hours to have their afternoons to play. Then dinner is crazy because they want to get their homework started or sit down and eat what I have cooked. They don't like the food I cook and prefer eating out more. So I have now found it easier to just run and pick up some fast food since that is all they will really eat anyway. Why waste time cooking if no one will eat it?"

As I listened to Suzy, I could hear that she was stuck and couldn't find her way to her new normal. I also knew what goals and action steps she needed to implement in both her financial and parenting life to move forward. You probably do as well:

- To receive financial coaching on budgeting
- To find employment—at least during school hours—to provide more income
- To sell the house and find something more affordable
- To get her focus off her ex-husband's parenting style and create her own boundaries and rules for her home
- To let go of the guilt and comparison with her ex-husband

That was enough to get started, and I told Suzy just that. I'd heard her challenges and goals, and I knew exactly which goals she needed to begin with and the action steps needed to take to reach success.

I gave her a notebook to begin tracking every dime she spent every day for thirty days, so we could put together a budget.

I told her to get her resumè finished and send it out to five prospective employers over the next two weeks.

I gave Suzy the name of three fantastic results-oriented realtors and told her to contact them for a consultation about selling her home. She could then select the right realtor.

I gave her a plan for how she should have the children eat a snack after school, complete 50 percent of their homework, which would earn them one hour of playtime, and then finish the rest of their work before dinner. (I also said she needed to start making dinner for them, both for budget necessity and health reasons.)

Finally, I told her to get their bags, clothes, and lunches ready the night before for the following day.

Our next two coaching sessions left me feeling very discouraged. Suzy hadn't taken a single action and didn't seem to realize how important it was for her to do the work and plan I had crafted.

Coaching the Coach Tip

It is easy for a coach to see the big picture for our clients. We are trained, skilled, and insightful, and when we listen to our clients, we can often move ahead of them. That is exactly what I had done with Suzy. I knew what she needed to do, and my action steps were good, but they were mine. I'd moved ahead of my client.

From coaching Suzy, I learned that the vision and goals have to be the client's and not the coach's, even if those goals will not produce the results the client is seeking as quickly. The action steps must also be ones the client has actively participated in creating, to ensure "buy-in." Once I began to coach Suzy to find her own answers and process, I began to see her commitment, and she experienced real progress.

Referring Out
Pam Taylor

It is not doing the thing we like to do, but
liking the thing we have to do, that makes life blessed.
Johann Wolfgang von Goethe

Abigail* was my favorite client ever—what a delight she was. I looked forward to every call because she had so much life and joy. She saw God everywhere and loved to create beauty from nothing. She was always on time for her calls and never skipped sending a prep form the day before her appointment. The perfect client.

Here's how it started: She'd searched the Internet for Christian coaches and found me. She had many questions. She'd heard about Christian coaches and so she wanted to understand what a coach could do for her. She had been an entrepreneur for three years but wasn't making any money. She wanted help with her self-confidence.

I learned that Abigail was a creator of clay pots. A gifted lady, she did beautiful work. As well, she was an expert in advertising on social media sites. A delight to work with, I loved coaching her for months.

She would often speak of how difficult it was to get along with her husband, but it sounded like it was just that he didn't understand her need to create. He was a practical man. He viewed it as a waste of time and money to have her involved in "that foolishness."

Their problems seemed like normal misunderstandings. She said that they were being mentored by an older Christian couple. It seemed to be moving along slowly, but at least she was proactive about it. And she went to church regularly and had close Christian friends. I wasn't worried.

She told me sad stories about her abusive childhood. I could understand her deep need to create beauty. I suggested she take the Sacred Pathways assessment to understand more about her particular worship style as a way for her to connect more deeply with God. Understanding our Creator's design helped her become more in tune with Him. She was delighted. It brought her into closer fellowship with God.

She discovered that she draws closer to God through her senses and through nature. That helped her see why she got inspired with new creative ideas when she was outside.

She began to grow in confidence and had opportunities to show her work. When she did, people liked and bought it. That was cause for celebration. Life was good. It looked as if we would be in coach/client relationship for a long time. It was working the way it is supposed to.

Then, at the end of one of her calls, she said she wanted to discuss her greatest fears—next time. Not that day.

Before our next session, I received the fateful prep form: "My husband and I struggled last week. He was physically aggressive with me. I'm experiencing occasional chest pains—doctor ordered an EKG and stress test for me." I also learned that her husband had threatened to take her youngest daughter away from her. Reading some additional comments on her prep form, I made a note: "Those phrases seem to be cries for help for which I am not trained."

I contacted a fellow coach for moral support and to confirm what I believed to be the right thing to do. This was a sad decision for me to have to make but I had to refer out and end the coaching relationship. I was not qualified to help her with what she needed most. This was an adult decision I could not base on my feelings.

Abigail and I began her final call with prayer and then had a difficult conversation.

Coaching the Coach Tip

From Christopher McCluskey, my mentor coach, and in the classes I'd taken with the Christian Track of ILCT and also in classes at Professional Christian Coaching Institute (PCCI), I'd been taught what to do when we need to refer out to someone else when a client needs a different kind of help than we can give them. But knowing what to do and doing it are two entirely different things.

I'd loved working with Abigail. We'd made such headway. I didn't want to lose her as a client, but I had to do what was right for her. As Rick Warren writes in *The Purpose Driven Life*, "It's not about me." That doesn't mean saying goodbye was easy. Not at all. I wept about what was happening to my sister-in-Christ, the pain she was experiencing with her husband, and the hard decisions she was going to have to make. And I wept over the loss of a dear client.

Abigail and I had our time of closure on that scheduled call. I prayerfully and gently told her why I had to refer her out. She understood and she agreed. I affirmed what a precious child of God she is. I made clear how much I had loved working with her, but that this was best for her. I also encouraged her to seek a safe place for her and her children.

I refunded her fee for the month and I sent a follow-up email to her, carefully documenting what we had discussed. I kept a copy and wrote a more detailed account for her permanent file, stating the thought processes that brought me to my decision to refer out.

I also contacted my coach to tell him the file was closed, and I had done the hard thing. He understood. He was proud of me.

Closure. Documenting the details. Saying goodbye. The right thing to do. But it was hard, so very hard to do.

With sadness I let her go as a coaching client, but also with love and support for her best interest.

* Names and identifying details were changed to protect the client's identity.

Chapter 10

Handling Challenging Clients

The definition of a challenging client is different for different coaches. Maybe challenging for you is a client whom you perceive as more intelligent or more credentialed than you are. One certified coach who was just launching her business did not have a master's degree. She was extremely uncomfortable when she discovered her first paying client was a professor at Princeton University with a Ph.D. When she focused on her client's goals, however, rather than the client's degrees, she was successful in helping her client move forward.

Don't lose sight of the fact that difficult clients can be wonderful opportunities for you to grow as a coach. Rather than believing that a great coach knows all the answers, believe that great coaches lean on a great God to guide them.

There is not one tool or technique that will always work with everyone.

When traditional coaching wisdom seems to fail, follow the wisdom outlined in Proverbs 3:5-7, "Trust God from the bottom of your heart; don't try to figure out everything on your own. Listen for God's voice in everything you do, everywhere you go; he's the one who will keep you on track. Don't assume that you know it all. Run to God!" (THE MESSAGE).

Maintaining Your Focus
Dr. Dave Martin

Think about things that are excellent and worthy of praise.
Philippians 4:8b NLT

What is the most important thing in becoming a winner?" Tony asked one Monday afternoon. His previous week had not gone well, and he was struggling.

I took a moment to reflect. This was the same question so many of my clients have asked. Senior pastors want to know the "breakthrough" point and how to achieve it. Business leaders are searching for the difference that will distinguish their company from the competition, and individual achievers look for the vital ingredient in becoming great.

After several moments, I said, "Tony, tell me about your week." And he did. In vivid detail, Tony enumerated his difficulties. As a NASCAR driver, Tony had strong competition, and it quickly became obvious that he was disgusted, disillusioned, and altogether distracted.

But he had seen fierce competition before and had not faltered. This was something new, and I needed to know more.

So I said, "Tony, I want to hear about your week again, but this time, please tell me what you were thinking each morning when you arrived at the track. Tell me where your thoughts led you throughout the day when you were driving and what your dominant thoughts were at night when you were home."

This took a bit more time as Tony mused over his previous week, but finally he started to talk.

"Dr. Dave, it's the wall." he said with an exasperated sigh. "All I can think about is the wall."

Tony went on to explain that the primary concern of all new racecar drivers is the wall. Nobody wants to hit the wall, especially at 200 miles per hour. He also explained that the centrifugal force of the automobile tends to propel the car directly toward the wall as the car speeds around the track. So the wall is a constant problem for all drivers, but for new drivers, it is the principal fear.

"Consequently," he explained, "the wall is all the new driver can think about. As he drives faster and faster, he keeps telling himself, 'Don't hit the wall. Don't hit the wall.'"

I stopped him there. "Tony," I asked, "When you are driving, as you circle the track, are you thinking about winning?"

"Not really—no. No, I'm not." He reflected more. "Right then, I'm just concentrating on not hitting the wall."

Tony had lost his focus. He had allowed his thoughts and fears to take his eyes off the primary objective of winning the race, and he had become focused instead on avoiding the wall.

NASCAR rookies are actually trained to turn their thoughts away from the wall and onto the infield. Rookie drivers quickly learn that you are drawn toward the thing that dominates your thoughts, and so they deliberately retrain their thinking to focus on the infield instead of the wall. Over time, their thoughts are concentrated on the infield, and as a result, the feeling that they are being pulled toward the wall as they speed around the track is drastically reduced and their crippling fear is disarmed. They become potential winners.

It took months for Tony to make the thought swap from the "wall" to the "win," but in time, he was able to redirect his thoughts and focus completely on his goal. He is now making headlines in the NASCAR world.

That Monday with Tony clarified a valuable lesson for me, too. In life, just as in NASCAR, we are dominated by the thoughts we choose. No matter what your profession or calling, your thought choice determines your focus, thus becoming the most critical element in your success.

Coaching the Coach Tip

Sometimes as coaches, we spend so much time working on the problems and issues of others that our own focus is lost. It's easy, both with clients and in our own lives, to concentrate on the problem and to lose sight of the win. I repeatedly tell my clients, "The key is to know your goal and not to be distracted by the peripherals. Keep your eyes on the prize. You are dominated by the thoughts you choose."

Our thoughts determine our focus, so like Paul's instruction to the Philippians, we should daily "think about things that are excellent and worthy of praise."

And know, "The rest of your life will be the best of your life!"

From Failure to Phenomenal
Lisa Gomez Osborn

Whenever two or three of you come together in
my name, I am there with you.
Matthew 18:20 CEV

I'll never forget my first coaching session with Jennifer; it was a complete disaster. At least, that's what I felt at the time. Jennifer, a tall, blonde, twenty-four-year-old woman, came for coaching after I had been professionally coaching for about two years. Our first session was one of the most awkward I have ever experienced.

Jennifer's personality emanated an unusual standoffishness, with almost a disdain for me. I found it perplexing and intimidating. Unfortunately, I began doing everything wrong. I tried to get her approval. I tried to get her to laugh. Nothing. Finally, out of ideas, I asked her why she had come to see me, which is what I should have asked when she first sat down.

Unbelievably, she shrugged her shoulders and said she didn't really know.

Okay, I thought, this is going to be the longest hour of my life. Determined to do a good job, I sat up straighter, put on my best "attentive coach" countenance and asked her the question I always ask whenever I'm completely baffled: "Will you tell me a little about yourself?"

Normally, people are good at talking about themselves, but not Jennifer. She frowned. "There's not really much to tell."

I waited.

Fortunately, she continued.

She told me she was a hairstylist, had flunked out of college, and now she was miserable.

At my request for more information, she said she had attended a private Catholic high school and had earned a full art scholarship to a private university. There, she explained, she was so anxious about being rebuffed by her professors she couldn't approach them when she began having academic problems. Instead, she opted to stop attending classes. Eventually she flunked her first-year courses, and her scholarship was retracted.

She then moved back home with her mom and her mom's boyfriend, who she said she detested. To make matters worse, she stated that she wanted to bring her mom in for our next session for relationship and communication coaching.

That revelation was a shock. I had been hoping that this session would be our first and last. Surprisingly, she made a second appointment.

"Oh, by the way," I said as she was leaving, "here's a book on setting boundaries in relationships that you might want to read before our next session."

Our second appointment was nearly as bad as our first. Before I could even say hello, she pulled the book out of her bag and tossed it onto my desk. "I read the whole thing in one evening and didn't learn a thing," she said.

Oh dear, I thought. I felt like an idiot and wondered if I was intellectually inferior because I hadn't been able to read that book in one night.

But I put on my figurative coaching hat and we began. Since this session was with Jennifer and her mother, we spent our time discussing their relationship and what they each wanted to get out of coaching. It was not pretty.

After they left, I was exhausted, discouraged, and ready to refer them to someone else.

Before our next session, I discussed the case with my own life coach. Truthfully, I needed help and wanted my coach to tell me what to do. Of course, she didn't. Instead, she suggested we pray.

While we were praying, God brought a fact to my mind. I had forgotten that Jennifer's mom was into the New Age movement and believed in a "higher power." This case is spiritual warfare, I thought. This idea completely shifted my thought process about Jennifer and how to proceed with her, and it reminded me of the critical urgency of taking every client before the Lord.

Over the course of the next nine sessions, Jennifer slowly began to transform before my eyes. I referred her to a psychiatrist as well, and her mom returned for two more sessions.

The changes in Jennifer were amazing. During one critical session, she mentioned that her father had been wounded in the Vietnam War. That revelation set off a chain of questions, which eventually led to us realizing that Jennifer was eligible to go to any college in the state for free.

Jennifer and her mom's relationship also underwent dramatic change. At the beginning of our coaching sessions, each one had stated that the relationship was poor and the two couldn't talk without fighting. The mother felt that Jennifer was a slob and didn't help at all around the house, and Jennifer felt that her mother favored the boyfriend over their mother-daughter relationship and never wanted to spend any time with her. During one session, they made a commitment to have a mother-daughter-only date two times a month. Because Jennifer received some much-needed attention and affirmation from her mother, she began to want to help around the house; she even organized her room, the laundry room, and the entire second floor, a subject that had previously been a serious source of contention between the two.

Jennifer's interest in art also returned. She hadn't drawn or painted since she had flunked out of college. After coaching, she enrolled in college, began selling her artwork, and started earning straight A's. She was elated about her returning creativity. She even quit smoking, went back to eating a vegetarian diet, and lost twenty-five pounds.

Jennifer became less anxious—another huge change. Prior to coaching, she never left home without her prescription anti-anxiety medication, Xanax, because of daily panic attacks. "You'll never guess what," she told me during one session. "I haven't had a Xanax in a month. And I haven't even bothered to refill my prescription." She smiled from ear to ear. "I never imagined I'd be able to do without it."

In our last session, Jennifer described an "emergency" with a friend. She had tried to contact me for help, but when she wasn't able to get in touch with me, she realized she could come up with her own solution. She remembered something from the book I had loaned her on setting healthy boundaries and established some boundaries on a friendship that had been very lopsided. In doing so, she gained incredible confidence.

As she told me this, I felt like a proud mama hen.

I'm a much better coach because of having my own coach. I thought this particular client was going to be disastrous for me, and I was ready to give up. It's very likely that I'd never have been able to have the objectivity crucial to a successful coaching relationship with Jennifer if I hadn't had my own coach. I'm so thankful for her. Had I tried to figure out this difficult client on my own, I might have missed an excellent opportunity to make a difference in her life. I would not have experienced the pervasively positive influence that can be transmitted through the coaching relationship, and I would have missed experiencing the vital guidance that prayer exerts in every coaching session and relationship.

Coaching the Coach Tip

Don't give away or give up on a difficult client too soon. Contact another coach for additional perspective. Above all, remember to take the situation to the Lord in prayer, preferably with that other coach.

I now look at difficult clients differently. Instead of seeing them as draining or as a burden, I see the relationship as an opportunity for them and me to grow. They are God's hidden treasures. I just need to separate my emotions and thoughts from theirs. Rather than thinking I'm not coaching well enough or I'm an idiot, I need to ask God to shift my perspective and show me how I can best benefit them.

When You Don't Know What to Do
Kim Avery

Trust in the Lord with all your heart
And do not lean on your own understanding.
In all your ways acknowledge Him,
And He will make your paths straight.
Proverbs 3:5-6 NASB

I got off the phone with Jeanette and laid my head in my hands. My biggest fear had just come true. Going into career coaching had been a bad idea.

How had I gotten myself into this?

Back in November 2006, when I decided to lay aside my counseling practice to train as a life coach, it seemed like a good move. Working daily with people on their life mission, purpose, and goals would provide me with the perfect combination of challenge and exhilaration.

And it did. Each day was a new adventure, and each new client confirmed that I had made the right choice. In fact, I loved it so much that three years later I decided to dive in even deeper; I signed up for additional training in career coaching.

My small career coaching class of eight had seven full-time career professionals who wanted to learn to coach along with me, a coach who knew nothing about careers. Three minutes into the class, they were already speaking a language I didn't understand. Writing resumès, interviewing, networking, accessing the hidden-job market, and more were common classroom topics, but ones I knew nothing about.

While my career-oriented classmates worked hard to move themselves from consulting mode to a coaching role, I swam the opposite direction trying to fill my head with volumes of career-specific information.

Week after week, my instructor assured us (me) that as coaches we didn't need to be an expert in everything. Our job was to coach the clients and allow them to discover the answers on their own.

I nodded, smiled, ignored her, and kept swimming upstream. There was so much information available, and I had convinced myself that I needed to know it all.

The thirty hours of instruction flew by. I survived the class, passed the test, and received my career coach certification. To the outsider, it all looked good. Internally, I was a nervous wreck, convinced there was still more I needed to know.

Two weeks later, Jeanette, my first career-coaching client, arrived on my virtual doorstep.

Jeanette's tone of voice attested to her discouragement as she shared her dilemma. Recently divorced, Jeanette was unexpectedly faced with being her family's sole breadwinner. Money was tight. She needed a job, and she needed it right away.

Unfortunately, her work history was limited. Jeanette had worked briefly for an insurance agency prior to her first child being born. Before that, well, there was no before that. Those few short years of clerical work was all the employment experience she had.

But that was only the first of many obstacles.

Just six months prior to her divorce, Jeanette had been diagnosed with a seizure disorder. While it rarely interfered with her everyday activities, she was no longer allowed to drive.

Jeanette was stranded at home, and the closest town was more than twenty miles away. There was no bus. She couldn't afford a cab. She had no local friends, and her family wouldn't help. She couldn't afford to move because she didn't have a job, but, of course, she didn't have a job because she needed to move.

She saw no way out, and I agreed. Not out loud, of course. But with each new piece of information Jeanette revealed, my heart sank deeper and deeper into my chest.

My private nightmare had come true. She was looking to me for answers. I had none. Becoming a career coach had been a very, very big mistake.

The hour ended quickly. Outwardly optimistic, I set up her next appointment, but inwardly I was praying that the Lord would come before we met again.

Later that week, I poured out my tale of woe to my own coach. "So you can see," I said, as I finished describing Jeanette's catch-22, "she's trapped. There is no answer, and there's nothing I can do." I paused, waiting for my coach to agree.

Instead, I heard a gentle chuckle on the other end of the phone. "You are getting hooked by her description. That's her perspective. There are other perspectives. There always are."

I agreed that normally that might be the case, but in this instance, Jeanette was the exception that proved the rule.

Hearing my skepticism, my coach pressed on.

Answering her powerful questions, I reviewed the things I absolutely knew to be true:

- God is all-powerful.
- God is good.
- God loved Jeanette.
- God had provision for her life.

The more I talked the more I realized how my own insecurities as a career coach had gotten in the way of coaching Jeanette. I assumed that since I couldn't think of any answers that meant there weren't any.

It was time to remind myself of the basics:

- The coach doesn't need to know the answers, and a positive outcome doesn't depend on the coach.

- The coach just needs to coach and believe in what God can do.

With renewed faith, I approached my next coaching call with Jeanette with great anticipation. While her circumstances were still bleak, I was different. Freed from having to know the answers, I asked all new questions. And through those faith-filled questions, the Holy Spirit brought possibilities to Jeanette's mind—lots of possibilities.

Perhaps she could work from home. Or maybe her cousin, who needed a place to live, might be willing to give Jeanette a ride to work in exchange for a bedroom. Jeanette and the kids might be able to live temporarily with a friend in town, or this might be the time to experiment with the new medication her doctor wanted to try. The list went on and on.

Both Jeanette and I left her second session renewed, invigorated, and excited to see what God was going to do. And God provided, as He always does.

I'm so thankful for my time with Jeanette because it reminded me that I don't have to know the answers. I just need to know the God who does. Maybe becoming a career coach wasn't such a bad idea after all.

Coaching the Coach Tip

It's natural to feel insecure when we are doing something new. After years of counseling and coaching, I still find insecurity bubbling up at unexpected times. It's a normal human emotion and one that we can't prevent.

Thankfully, there is never any need to worry when we don't have the answers. We aren't supposed to. Our firm foundation of faith in God and His willingness to work through the coaching process moves our clients forward more than any manmade solution ever could.

Does Your Creative Client Need Creative Strategies?
Jennifer Cisney Ellers

The world is full of people that have stopped listening to themselves or have listened only to their neighbors to learn what they ought to do, how they ought to behave, and what the values are that they should be living for.
Joseph Campbell

The lessons and applications that work with many of my coaching clients do not work with my artistic clients. While goal setting, organization, discipline, and focus can be helpful, I have not found these tools to be tremendously helpful in fostering creativity in creative right-brain types looking for help in many aspects of their lives and careers.

Kate had loved writing since she was a child. Though she had a successful career in sales, she always considered writing to be her true passion and her true occupation. She hoped one day she could focus more time and energy on writing.

When she married at age thirty-one, her husband suggested she work part time and spend the extra time writing. She was thrilled and excited to get started. What she didn't anticipate was that she would be faced with a huge case of writer's block. It seemed as if the creative ideas that had been flowing continuously through her brain for years had suddenly dried up the moment she sat down at her computer to record them.

Since I am a life coach and also have an undergraduate degree in journalism, a mutual friend referred Kate to me.

I like my clients to start with an honest assessment of their talent. After all, it is not helpful to encourage clients to pursue a field in which they simply don't have the talents or skills to be at least moderately successful.

184

Kate sent me some articles and short stories she had written in the past. They were insightful, interesting, and easy to read. She had both talent and a passion for writing. Now, she finally had the time to write, but her dream was not working as she had envisioned.

We started with some standard wisdom. She sought out an upcoming writers workshop in her area. She would attend for inspiration and direction. In the meantime, she set aside chunks of uninterrupted time each week to write. She created a space in her home to focus on her writing and eliminated distractions (turning off her cell phone, closing email, etc.).

I wish I could tell you she got instant success. No. In fact, things got worse. A teacher at the writers workshop offered the solution that writers should write something every day whether or not they felt inspired or creative. I thought this was great advice and echoed this to Kate.

She wrote, but she told me what she wrote was terrible.

"You're probably being too critical," I said. "Why don't you send it to me so I can assess it?"

She was right. It was terrible. It was disjointed, flat, and lacking the insight and overall sparkle of her previous work. The more Kate implemented the disciplines suggested, the worse her writing became.

"Tell me how you feel when you are writing now," I asked Kate in one of our phone sessions.

"The same way I feel when I do laundry," she replied.

I didn't have to question that response because I knew she hated doing laundry. It was her least favorite household chore. After some discussion, it became clear that the more discipline we instituted in Kate's practice of writing, the less she enjoyed it. At least for Kate, joyless writing led to bad writing.

"Now that I feel like I have to write," she said, "I don't want to write. I'm forcing myself to sit down at my computer and type something, but I'm not really feeling inspired."

As her coach, I had to reevaluate my approach. I believe success in any aspect of life requires a combination of discipline and passion. But there is a delicate balance between the two. When we focus too much on what we should do, we can lose what we desire to do. When that happens, we lose our creative spark.

During our next coaching session, we focused on what Kate loved about writing and the circumstances under which she experienced her highest levels of creativity. Kate discovered her writing thrived when she felt relaxed and not pressured to write. So we decided she should stop writing, or at least stop putting it on her to-do list. I instructed her to focus her time and energy elsewhere, working on a long list of things she needed to do—anything but writing. Amazingly, as soon as the pressure to write was off, her desire to write came back.

Kate realized that her creativity showed up when she did not feel forced to write as a task but when it was a fun activity she could do after her daily tasks were completed.

Coaching the Coach Tip

I learned a valuable lesson from Kate, both as a coach and a person. Sometimes my clients do require focus and discipline. I need to hold them accountable to do what they need to do to meet their goals. But sometimes discipline isn't the issue. Sometimes they need permission to cut themselves some slack. And sometimes it's essential we design some creative strategies to meet their distinctive challenges.

The key lesson is that each of our coaching clients is a unique individual with a unique challenge. All helping professionals can fall into a rut where we expect the same techniques and tools to work for everyone. If we take time to really get to know our clients and their personalities, we will be more effective coaches. Sometimes the best action a coach can take is to challenge traditional wisdom and guide a client toward what works for him or her.

Conquering Cookie-Cutter Coaching
Linda Goldfarb

Obstacles don't have to stop you. If you run into a wall, don't turn around and give up. Figure out how to climb it, go through it, or work around it.
Michael Jordan

I met Robert, a 51 year old data entry technician, from Akron, Ohio, at a writer's conference two years before we began our coaching journey together. Robert's aspiration to be an "exceptional" speaker despite his early childhood diagnosis as a slow-learner has served as a barrier-blaster for me as a coach and the clients I've coached since then.

As a presentation coach, I usually work with high achieving individuals who desire to take their stage performance to the next level. They want more gigs, more repeat gigs, more laughs by adding appropriate humor, more audience interactions or a combination of some of these. With this default mindset, I tend to be several steps ahead of each client, carefully contemplating their possibilities and probabilities in preparation of the goals and desires they haven't even shared with me yet. In simplified terms, taking a presentation from muted to entertaining or mundane to humorous, typically requires similar steps fitted to the personality and purpose of the speaker, easy peasie—but Robert was not my usual client.

Robert is an inspirational motivator who speaks outside-the-box encouragement helping individuals with mental and or physical limitations to move beyond life's insecurities and disabilities. Our coaching relationship transpired via email and phone meetings. He sent me videos of his presentations to evaluate before accepting the coaching job, and I went to work immediately. Mentally critiquing the obvious mistakes and writing down my ideas of how he could perfect his talk to be more appealing to the audience, I felt adequately prepared for our initial phone coaching assessment session.

As with all of my clients, I opened the conversation with, "Robert, tell me what your goals are for our coaching relationship. Where do you want to be when we finish our journey?"

"I want to be the best speaker God made me to be and to tell others they can do anything they want as long as they don't give up."

Try as I might to pull more specific goals from Robert with questions like, "Do you want to increase your speaking gigs? Do you want to add humor into your talks? Would you be comfortable interacting more with the audience?" His simple desire to be a man of excellence for the Lord trumped everything. When we finished our conversation, I told Robert I needed to consider his expectations and that I would get back with him within a week.

Seriously, I considered not taking him on as a client due to the apparent communication barrier. As I continued to justify in my mind that I wasn't the right coach for Robert, God spoke into my heart, "Robert is the right coach for you."

"When the student is ready, the coach will come." Yeah, this wasn't exactly what I had in mind but, after prayerful deliberation, my choleric know-it-all mind finally got what the Lord was saying. His children are unique and gifted according to His will, and I don't serve cookie-cutter clients.

I contacted Robert as promised. We met by phone every two weeks; he shared his desires, and we slowly developed a game plan to meet his goals. I didn't push or heavily suggest; I clarified and offered options. Robert chose new steps, which was very exciting to me, and for three months, we traveled together tweaking his solo presentation of "Tiny Boxes."

My desire to be efficient and ahead of the coaching game had actually blocked my mind to God's promise for my clients by inserting my desires for them. Breaking down that barrier has transformed my coaching attitude from "Walk this way" to "Let's walk together" blessing my business and my clients beyond measure.

In the end, it was Robert's written challenge to his audience that reaffirmed the new direction of my coaching. Allow me to end with how he concludes his talk:

> "I challenge you to apply what you learned in today's session concerning the four steps.
>
> 1. Recognize your invisible boxes for what they are, unfounded confinement.
> 2. Agree to change your thinking to move beyond the box.
> 3. Explore the opportunities beyond your old thinking.
> 4. Take action to live your life with confidence."

Coaching the Christian Coach Tip

Be alert to your style of coaching and ask yourself, "Have I become so comfortable with my assessment tools or have my clients become so predictable that I've stopped seeing their unique needs?"

Your clients come to you because you offer them hope of success. Success does not rest on your shoulders alone but on the persistent collaboration between you, your client, and your Lord. Step out in confidence because He who began a good work in you will be faithful to complete it.

Big Hearts and Big Guns
Dr. Jennifer Degler

Above all else, guard your heart,
for everything you do flows from it.
Proverbs 4:23

I have a very strict gun control policy: if there's a
gun around, I want to be in control of it.
Clint Eastwood

Many of the business owners and professionals I coach have big hearts. They are Christians who genuinely love and care for other people; however, they often are stymied by their inability to grow their business. They are working very hard, putting in long hours, and managing multiple employees, yet their bottom line isn't improving, and their employees are underperforming. What's going wrong?

This was Carla's question to me as we began our coaching relationship. She owned a real estate agency in a large city and enjoyed serving on the board of a crisis-pregnancy center. With more than twenty years of experience in her field, she knew her industry well, but she was overwhelmed by a disorganized office, unmotivated employees, unmet goals, and overdue bills.

As Carla shared her story, my mind went in several directions. Should we tackle the disorganization piece first? Should I ask about financial procedures? Did she need to reevaluate her goals? I'm a practical, let's-jump-right-in kind of coach, but over the years, God has taught me to slow down and listen as the client tells me who she is, what she values, and often, what she needs to clarify first to bring about necessary movement and change. What do you learn from the following statements Carla made?

- "I want to use the money I earn to help people. I give a lot of money away."

- "I need to be more honest with people and myself in the moment, but I am afraid of being seen as mean or selfish."

- "I have six or seven employees, but it's like a revolving door. It's hard to build a business up and keep it going with the turnover."

- "I try to help my employees better themselves, but it's like they don't want to be more successful. Even with incentives, they don't meet agreed-upon goals."

- "I have trouble holding people accountable for what they need to do."

- "If an employee has a friend or relative who is in trouble and needs a job, I will often hire him or her. I try to give people a chance just like I was given a chance many years ago."

- "I hired my sister because she needed a job, but now I think she's missing work because she's using drugs. But I can't fire my own sister."

Clearly, Carla is a generous woman who highly values helping other people and giving them the same opportunities she once received. She has a big heart, and it's leading her to confuse ministry with business—a common problem for Christian business owners. She's made a practice of hiring people with problems in an effort to minister to them, a noble sentiment but one that is certain to torpedo her bottom line and frustrate her efforts to grow her business.

The "fix-it" part of me wanted to request that Carla immediately develop and implement a new set of management procedures that would produce a more professional and productive office. But clients with big hearts may find it difficult to implement new policies that seemingly conflict with their core value of helping others. Carla needed help first with clarifying and separating her personal mission from her business mission and then with reframing her new policies so that they once again honored her core values. In Carla's words, "If I follow through with more professional personnel decisions, my office will be more profitable, and then I'll have more money to give away to help others."

She worked hard to improve the professionalism in her agency, but she couldn't seem to take that final step of letting underperforming long-term employees go, and in particular, firing her sister who had refused a drug test. Final steps such as this bring big-hearted clients face to face with their fear of being seen as mean and selfish. If they are believers, then they may also fear that they will be viewed as a bad example of Christian love.

Big hearts paralyzed by big fears call for big guns. Big gun coaching techniques, that is. I don't pull out these types of techniques right off the bat in a coaching relationship because they work best when there is mutual trust and respect, and this takes time to develop. You'll know a technique feels like a big gun to your client if they react with a gulp, widened eyes, and perhaps a surprised utterance like, "Wow," "Oh my," or an expression that translates as "You are one crazy coach." (Just kidding about that last example.) You are suggesting a course of action that significantly raises the stakes, be they financial, emotional, physical, and so on. This will cause your client anxiety, which is why you need to establish a good working relationship first.

After three months of coaching, Carla and I trusted and respected each other. She acknowledged that she needed to fire her sister. She wanted to fire her sister. She could even see how this step might ultimately help her sister face her drug problem, but she needed help in pulling the trigger.

Finally, I asked her, "What organization would you least like to donate money to?" She immediately answered, "Planned Parenthood." As we spoke on the phone, I had her write out a check to Planned Parenthood, and she committed to mailing the check to them if she didn't fire her sister by a certain date and time. I reminded her that once Planned Parenthood received her check, she would forever be on their mailing list and would be listed online and in their materials as a financial supporter.

She fired her sister right on schedule.

Coaching the Coach Tip

Big-hearted clients often confuse ministry with business. You will get much better buy-in, follow-through, and lasting change if you first guide them to clarify and separate their personal mission and their business mission. Next, help them reframe new decisions so that these support their core value of helping others. And if they can't seem to get past the fear of being seen as mean or selfish, reach for a big-gun technique.

Chapter 11

Releasing or Ending a Coaching Relationship

Sometimes a client terminates the coaching relationship or maybe even "fires" his or her coach. Sometimes we as coaches make that choice because the client really needs a professional counselor or there is a clash of values.

But quite often there is mutual agreement between the coach and client that the client is ready to move on. Regardless of how the decision is reached, what is most important is that the ending is handled in a professional manner. Celebrate the client's progress and if possible, keep the door open for working together again in the future, if and when the client chooses to do so.

Bye for Now
Cheryl Scanlan

There is an appointed time for everything.
And there is a time for every event under heaven—
A time to give birth and a time to die;
A time to plant and a time to uproot what is planted.
Ecclesiastes 3:1-2 NASB

In the past month, two former clients reinitiated their coaching relationships after a six-month and two-year lapse respectively. I was pleasantly surprised that they were eager to reengage. My goodbyes used to be more difficult as I would secretly hang my head in shame wondering if I had served my client well. Over time, however, I learned how to develop stronger relationships through the separation process with clients. In the two instances mentioned above, our former coaching relationships were strong and viable, ending with clear invitations to continue if and when they felt it was time.

While either the client or the coach can decide it's time to say goodbye, through the years I've noticed a few clues that indicate the coaching relationship is nearing completion.

Clues From the client

- Coming to sessions indicating there wasn't much new to work on

- Pattern of not following through with designated actions

- Life gets in the way of living, such as family illness, where the client's emotional, physical, and/or intellectual energy is being maxed out from some ongoing concern

- Sense of accomplishment and readiness to branch off on own
- Specialized area of expertise required that is beyond the scope of current coaching relationship
- Situation arises that warrants consideration of counseling for a term
- Financial situation changes

Clues From the Coach's Viewpoint

- Relationship no longer fresh; rhythm turns to rote
- Not sensing "gaps" the client can move into or the next steps they could take
- Life gets in the way and circumstances hinder coach's ability to be fully present when interacting with client
- Unable, for whatever reason, to support the client in obtaining his or her objectives/goals
- Sense client has come to a place of completion or that it's time to encourage client to step out without the support and accountability of the coach

Each client is unique and I've learned to individualize my approach for each situation. I've also learned that I have to be willing to risk possibly losing the coaching relationship in order for it to have the best chance of flourishing. Sometimes I have to be brave with questions like "How well is this coaching relationship serving you right now?" or "What would you like to see different in our relationship?" or "You are able to bring more to the table. What's stopping you from doing so?"

A Coach's Role is to Respect and Release

My coaching relationships have ended for myriad reasons. One ended because we were not a good fit. He wanted someone to help propel his business forward using some tactics that I could not be involved in, even from an objective coach perspective. It just did not sit right with me. I was able to acknowledge that his approach was beyond my comfort zone, therefore, I would not be able to support him in his endeavors. He agreed it would be good to find someone else who could "advance his cause" with him. We had a mutually happy parting of ways and I referred him to a business coach who I knew had a much higher risk tolerance than I and who worked aggressively with his clients.

Another coaching relationship ended when the client felt she was at a place of "calm movement." We had enjoyed a celebration call the previous week and she felt a sense of settledness. We closed out our relationship the following session. Several years later, she called to begin again. We worked together for a brief three-month period to get her on track with a few more things.

One of the most awkward endings came with a client who was not following through with designed actions. Because he remained stuck throughout our sessions, I invested in sessions with a mentor to discern how I could better support this client. Eventually it became clear that the coaching was not serving him well. Whether it was my coaching style or something else was not "clicking," we both knew that coaching with me was not a good fit for him. We are, however, still in communication to this day.

Another time I said goodbye was when I needed a respite. I went through a brief period of significant health challenges. I informed my clients that, for a time, I needed to focus on taking care of myself to a greater degree. I did not have to end the relationships, but clients agreed to take a break or reduce to monthly sessions during this period. They appreciated and responded well to my concern for preserving the integrity of the coaching relationship on their behalf.

Celebration is a key component of the coaching relationship and the release. A coach's role is also to acknowledge and celebrate. No matter what is happening, a client needs to be acknowledged for the investment and the work they did. Sometimes I was so focused on the next stage, the next area of growth, I would leave my client panting in the dust as they attempted to "Whoa" the horsey. Again— my insecurity and desire to make sure the client got all the value I could give actually shortchanged the relationship. Less, I learned, is oftentimes better.

Celebration is equally important in releasing a client. Commemorate the challenges they successfully faced and the progress they made.

An open door and trust bring clients back. For instance, Christy shared that there was less for her to work on and she was feeling pretty good about where she was, but at the same time she didn't want to stop coaching. For the last couple of sessions, I felt like she was hanging on, but she had no current need for coaching.

I considered our options. What if she knew she could come back to coach whenever an opportunity arose again? We could transition to once a month for a couple of months and then finish for a season. This proposal was appropriate because as the coach, I manage the process while the client manages the objectives.

Christy seemed relieved by the suggestion. After three months she was off and running on her own. Two years later, she called and we were coaching again.

It is fun to walk with clients—some for a year and some for longer. But I can tell you there is still something special about a client calling me several years later ready to reengage in our coaching relationship.

Coaching the Coach Tip

An open door and trust encourage clients to re-initiate their coaching relationship, as does the unusual policy of holding my current coaching fees stable for two years after the end of the last session. If, for example, a client's fee was $150 a session and I've raised my fee to $175, his or her rate for the next two years, after we said goodbye, would still be $150.

Grandfathering in fees does create a bit of a bookkeeping nightmare, but I believe it is easier (and less expensive) to keep a client than it is to develop a client. I want my policies to reflect the value of returning business. Additionally, I do not have the preliminary work with a returning client. We step right back into coaching—another win-win incentive for the grandfather clause. Not all coaching practices share this policy, but I have worked this way for seven years and find it quite rewarding.

Unrepentant and Unwilling
Dr. Katie Brazelton

Repent, and turn from your sins. Don't let them destroy you!
Ezekiel 18:30b NLT

Over the past several decades as a Life Purpose Coach® and LifePlan facilitator, I've heard more sad stories from clients than my heart can bear at times. I've grieved, for example, with a woman who accidentally backed a car over her toddler sister years earlier. I've helped others whose homes and church had flooded, whose spouse had cheated, whose childhood was ripped away by sexual abuse, whose parents had moved thirty-two times, whose businesses and ministries had failed, whose brother had hanged himself, and whose child was terminally ill.

From these types of intense coaching sessions, I've come to understand that God can take any life story and turn it into a soul-winning testimony for His glory. In fact, my all-time favorite client is a fifty-six-year-old woman whose most frequently used words and expressions were the likes of, "I, me, my, mine, princess, queen bee, daddy's girl, it's all about me, and it's my way or the highway." When her pattern of pride became obvious to her in our conversations, she wept like a baby, thanked God for revealing the truth to her, and immediately asked Him for forgiveness.

But no client has ever caused me more consternation than a woman whom I'll call Sandy. I first met this married ministry leader over the phone when she called me on her pastor's recommendation. He suggested she talk to me about enlarging her ministry role at church, based on my perception of God's unique plan for her life. I was impressed by Sandy's servant's heart in my pre-screening interview and felt honored to accept her as a client.

The big day arrived for our first appointment, which I decided would be at my home to make the experience as lovely as possible for her. I had huge sunflowers smiling on the entryway table, an eclectic array of china preset on the dining room table for tea and biscotti, and the drapes opened wide to capture the lake view. I was prayed up and had prayer partners covering us.

The doorbell rang, and as I met Sandy on the front porch, she said, "I'm so glad I'm here." We were off to a great start in my doorway, until she blurted out, "I want to talk to you because my daughter married beneath herself." I was stunned. Where was the sweet Sandy? I braced myself for a tough session and once again asked God to guide me.

As she signed my guest book in the entryway, she made this announcement: "I just came from lunch at the yacht club."

Okay, no big deal. She was probably trying to make small talk, based on getting a glimpse of the lake outside my windows, but I did make a mental note to watch for signs of Better-Than-You Syndrome and Pay-Attention-to-Me Disease.

Off we went to the dining room table. I hadn't even finished doctoring up my tea; we hadn't even opened our coaching session in prayer, when out of the blue, Sandy shared with a grin, "I'm in love with a married dentist." Oh, man, what was I supposed to do with that?

Let me spare you the gory details about her intentions to have an affair with the dentist, with whom she'd just had lunch at the club. I'll even spare you the two sermonettes I gave her about adultery. I used every probing question, listening skill, intercessory prayer, and exhortation I could think of, to no avail. Sandy was not budging from her stubborn disregard for God's commandments, yet she had come seeking His will for her life. So I did what I had to do. I moved her to the living room for a change of scenery, tempo, and tone, mainly so I wouldn't be tempted to "guilt trip" her or to give up before God released me from the coaching session.

I was convinced that my new strategy would work. All I had to do was get her talking about God's call on her life; then I could circle back around and calmly ask her how an affair and ensuing ministry scandal would affect God's magnificent plans for her. I didn't let on about my mastermind intentions, and she didn't suspect a thing in my stealth approach.

Boy, did she light up like a Christmas tree when we discussed her "one big thing" that God had called her to do. When I realized, though, that her primary motives for wanting to know her "thing" were to satisfy her curiosity and for bragging rights, not follow-through, my intuition told me to redirect the session toward character formation. Then I felt like I had her just where I wanted her with the repentance deed being all but done; soon she'd be sobbing tears of remorse in my arms, so I resolved to stay the current course.

But my plan of circling back around to her affair was foiled; she never did bend, break, weep, or show any sign of concern about her emotional affair. At that point, my spirit was so grieved that I could barely contain my sorrow. I heard God asking me to stop the sham, and He called to mind the words of my personal LifePlan facilitator, Tom Paterson, who'd written *Living the Life You're Meant to Live*. Tom's voice in my head was saying, Stop. Don't participate in the mockery she's making of God's will. If she's unwilling to walk away from her sin, she's unwilling, and there's nothing you can do about it. Make no apologies for ending the session now.

Oh, Lordy Mercy, I didn't know if I had the wherewithal to be a tough-love coach. Thoughts rushed through my mind like a raging river: Where did I go wrong as a coach? What will she tell her pastor? How will I ever explain this difficult situation to the coaches I train? She's paid me quite handsomely. Do I owe her a refund?

I watched myself stand up tall and heard myself say to her calmly, "Sandy, we need to end our session now. I'd be happy to suggest the name of a Christian therapist who can help you see the spiritual danger you're in, but I can't coach you anymore. I strongly urge you to pull yourself out of ministry immediately. If you're willing to be honest with your pastor, I'll help you prepare for that meeting." (Pause. Inhale. Exhale.) "Let me walk you to the door."

We parted cordially, and I never heard from her again. I've replayed that coaching session dozens of times in my mind, looking for what I could have done differently, but I'm still stymied.

I pray you'll find countless ways to help countless clients turn their lives around for God, and I pray that you'll have the wisdom and courage to walk away from those who are unrepentant and even unwilling to discuss truth.

Coaching the Coach Tip

Strive to be a humble, non-judgmental, Luke 15 coach for straying sheep—a coach who cares deeply about sinners and remembers, "there is joy in the presence of God's angels when even one sinner repents" (Luke 15:10 NLT). But here's a good rule to memorize: When a client shows no remorse for sin and is unwilling to even consider the truth, don't continue throwing pearls to swine. (See Matthew 7:6 NASB.) When God says, "Enough of that stubborn pride!"—refer the person to a counselor, who can take a more clinical approach about underlying causes for the client's ungodly, rebellious behavior.

And don't let a bad experience sour you. Keep doing excellent work for the Lord with those who desire biblically-based coaching.

Getting Over Getting Fired
Leslie Vernick

Success is not final, failure is not fatal: it is the courage to continue that counts.
Winston Churchill

I don't think I want to continue working with you," my coaching client said. "You are not meeting my expectations."

My heart sank. I was new to coaching, transitioning my counseling practice over to more coaching clients. We already had two sessions and I thought they had gone fairly well. But in a flurry of emails over the weekend, she was angry that I was not available to do a spot-coaching call when she needed it.

Throughout our communication about her disappointment, I validated her feelings but also tried to help her see that coaching was not synonymous with on-call help. In the intake, I sensed this person might be a little needy, but as I explained the difference between coaching and counseling, I thought she understood and was willing to work within the limits of our coaching relationship. But from her perspective, I failed to deliver what I'd promised and she no longer wanted to work with me.

Part of me felt relieved. One of the reasons I wanted to transition my practice to coaching was to have less stress. I also felt guilty and sad. Rejection is always painful and I asked myself over and over again, What could I have done differently? This experience also shook my confidence in my coaching abilities. Can I successfully make this transition? I wondered.

As I worked through my own feelings of failure, I realized that God could use what I learned to help my coaching clients deal with their failures, too. One of the most serious problems that keep people from making significant changes, reaching their dreams, or achieving their goals is how they process failure. Many of us get stuck because we're scared of falling down, or we stay stuck because we're unable to move past our pain, regrets, or guilt over past failures.

If you want to grow as a person and as a coach, however, it is absolutely critical that you be willing to try new things, embrace challenges, and pick yourself up when you fall down. I learned an important concept: Failure is not a statement about you. It's a statement about what happened.

Coaching the Coach Tip

Five lessons that helped me move through this failure in a healthy way:

1. Don't Give Up

Kathryn Stockett, author of The New York Times best-selling novel *The Help*, didn't give up writing her novel in spite of receiving sixty rejection letters. Rather than get discouraged after all those rejections, she got determined and reworked and rewrote her story, evaluating every critique and criticism to improve her writing.

What would have happened to her dream if she told herself, "I can't do it; I give up"? Thankfully, she persevered and the sixty-first letter she received was the acceptance letter.

There are many individuals throughout history who have pushed through rejection, failures, discouragement, and seemingly impossible odds. Abraham Lincoln is one of the most famous. After losing numerous elections as well as many personal setbacks, eventually he became the President of the United States and changed American history.

Inspired by examples like Kathryn Stockett and Abraham Lincoln, I decided I wasn't going to give up coaching, but I also had a lot to learn from this experience. We'll never know what could have been if we stop trying.

2. Take Responsibility

One of the most important skills we must learn is how to take responsibility for our choices and recalculate. Otherwise, we usually repeat the same mistakes again and again wondering why this is happening to us, often blaming others, God, and life circumstances instead of looking at ourselves.

To take responsibility for our own actions does not necessarily mean we take full blame for something, although this is often why many of us avoid taking responsibility. Perhaps a more helpful way of thinking about taking responsibility is to call it "ownership."

I asked myself, What part of this failure do I need to own? What part did I play? Things don't just happen to us. Taking responsibility for the part we play helps us make changes so that we don't repeat the same mistakes.

3. Stop Beating Yourself Up

Owning our mistakes is not the same thing as beating ourselves up for them. Taking responsibility helps us grow and learn. Beating ourselves up just makes us feel guilty and ashamed.

We all have regrets. Things that we wish we would have done or known. We must be able to get over them and move on. One of failure's lessons is accepting our limitations and making the adjustments needed to capitalize on our strengths.

4. Recognize You Have Blind Spots

When my daughter was first learning to drive, I warned her repeatedly to make sure she checked her mirrors and looked before she changed lanes. I didn't want her to get into an accident because she didn't realize that someone else's entire vehicle can hide in our car's blind spot.

People have blind spots, too. Once we recognize what ours are, we can be more careful and not take stupid risks.

Our biggest blind spots come from our own pride and self-deception. In hindsight, my gut feelings were telling me that this person would not make a good coaching client. But I was anxious to get new clients and in my pride I thought if I set the boundaries and worked on specific goals, she could make some progress in what she wanted to do. I should have listened to my gut and other experts who tell us how to determine who is a good fit for coaching and who is not.

5. Ask For Help

Once we can take responsibility and identify our personal blind spots, we realize that we need help and invite others to speak into our lives. Proverbs says, "Get all the advice and instruction you can, so you will be wise the rest of your life" (Proverbs 19:20 NLT).

No one becomes successful entirely on his own. All of the greatest leaders in the world had people behind and alongside them who helped them get there and encouraged them to get back up when they fell down. Do you think the Apostle Paul could have done all he did without the support and help from Barnabas, Timothy, or Titus?

We can surround ourselves with people who are a little further along on the journey than we are. Studies show that when people are looking to make a significant change, it helps to have the support of others who will cheer them on and bandage their bruises. For instance, I hired my own coach to help me learn coaching better.

Don't let failure stop you. Instead, you too can learn the necessary stepping-stones that will lead you to make the changes that lead to more success.

Entering the Danger Zone
Dr. Jennifer Degler

Do not worry beforehand about what to say. Just say whatever is given you at the time, for it is not you speaking, but the Holy Spirit.
Mark 13:11

You'll never see me cliff diving. I've never jumped out of an airplane, and there is no way I would even consider running with the bulls in Pamplona. Risk taker? Not me. Well, at least not when it comes to physical risks. But when it comes to taking risks as a coach, I have learned to jump out of the proverbial airplane whenever the Holy Spirit nudges me to enter the danger zone.

This lesson hasn't been easy to learn. As a beginner coach, many times I was so focused on trying to be brilliant that I completely missed His still, small voice. Hours after a coaching call, I would feel vaguely uneasy and wonder what I had missed. Gradually, as I learned to trust His nudges, I began to listen more to both my clients and the Holy Spirit. Listening resulted in my asking questions that were better overall for my client but may not have made much sense at first. The questions that ran the risk of offending or confusing my clients took me into the danger zone.

Don't be afraid to go boldly into the danger zone, particularly if you feel the Holy Spirit's prompting. You never know how God will use your obedience.

This truth was vividly illustrated in my coaching practice recently during a coaching call with Elizabeth, a longtime client. She is a Christian professional woman with a full-time job and a coaching practice on the side. Our sessions were primarily focused on building her coaching practice. I love coaching the coach and looked forward to our calls because of Elizabeth's creativity and enthusiasm. She is an endearing people-pleaser who struggles to set and maintain appropriate boundaries in her relationships. Her support network included her husband, who she described as "one of the good guys," a Christian man who encouraged her efforts to become a life coach.

We worked together for several months, and then Elizabeth took a break from coaching while she and her husband had a baby. Over the next couple of years, we worked together off and on as she adjusted to motherhood, started a new job, expanded her coaching practice, and tried to maintain a healthy work-life balance. I celebrated with her as she gained coaching clients, and I challenged her to ask for appropriate compensation because she undervalued herself and thus undercharged clients. We role-played appropriate assertiveness in her job setting and with coaching clients because she struggled at times to ask directly for what she wanted.

During our most recent call, as we were discussing how to enlist her husband's participation with more chores at home, she made the comment, "I tend to avoid conversations like that with him because he loses his temper sometimes." This was the first time in all the years we'd worked together that she had mentioned his temper. I remembered the many positive comments she had made about her husband but still felt this check in my spirit. Something didn't feel right. God was prompting me to go into the danger zone.

I didn't want to go there. I reminded myself, you are her coach, not her counselor. Don't ask counseling-type questions. I wondered if she would be offended when I was so off base with my questions. I pretty much had talked myself out of following up on the comment about her husband's temper.

Have you ever noticed how persistent the Holy Spirit can be?

Fine, I'll ask the awkward question so we can move on. "When your husband loses his temper, does he ever get so angry that he threatens, shoves, or hits you?"

I was stunned when Elizabeth said, "Yes." I expect to hear that admission when I am with counseling clients, but it never even really occurred to me that a coaching client, and in particular a coaching client who was a coach herself, could also be experiencing domestic abuse.

At that point, I had to switch from coaching to crisis intervention. At first, she said he hadn't hit her in a long time, but when questioned about specific dates, she admitted that just weeks earlier he had shaken her and slapped her across the face. This was also the first time he had abused her in front of their daughter, an escalation in the abuse cycle.

Once you and your clients go into the danger zone and see what's really going on, you can't go back and act like you don't know what you now know. You have to guide your clients to embrace the truth and make their decisions based on an accurate picture of reality. This may be painful for your client, and in this case, it was also painful for me as the coach. I had to tell her, gently but firmly, that her focus needed to be on her and her child's safety. I couldn't in good conscience continue to coach her about building her coaching practice while knowing that she, and possibly her child, were in danger. We also discussed the legalities of reporting spousal abuse in her state.

We decided to take a break from coaching as Elizabeth is focusing on getting counseling for domestic abuse and deciding what to do with her marriage. She has spoken with her pastor, who is supportive of her decision to ask her husband to live elsewhere while he receives treatment, and he has now moved out. I stay in contact with Elizabeth and have offered her three free coaching sessions when she is ready to get back into coaching. I don't typically offer clients free sessions, but I felt a persistent nudge from the Holy Spirit to do so. After this situation, I am even quicker to obey that still, small voice. You never know how God will use your obedience.

Coaching the Coach Tip

Go boldly into the danger zone when prompted by the Holy Spirit. Remember that people-pleasing clients who have trouble with issues such as being assertive, setting boundaries, asking for appropriate compensation, and understanding their value may have or have had an emotionally/physically/financially abusive person in their life such as a spouse, boss, or parent. While coaching's focus is not to unearth or dig deep to discover these issues, we cannot ignore that they can and do crop up; therefore, in the best interests of the client, they need to be addressed.

If you become aware that your client is being abused, remember to put safety first. A coaching client must be reasonably safe in order to truly make progress in building a new business. Otherwise, it's like putting a new roof on a house with a damaged foundation.

Walking the Fine Line
Mary Sorrentino

And this I pray, that your love may abound still more and
more in real knowledge and all discernment.
Philippians 1:9 NASB

Coaching clients often walk through trials and at times get stuck at pivotal points in life. Ann-Marie is bone-weary of visiting nursing homes and hospitals but cannot bring herself to ask her siblings to take over eldercare a few hours a week so she can take a long-desired painting class. Melissa's cycle of hopefulness while making suggestions and discouragement after her depressed husband shoots them down has resulted in her becoming more and more convinced God is not for her or for her marriage. I coach these women, and others just like them, who support loved ones in difficult life circumstances.

Whether your coaching niche is pastors or college students, many of your clients invariably will come to pivotal points when you have to decide if it's time to refer them to a counselor. In my niche, that decision point comes quite frequently.

Choosing a coaching niche was never a struggle for me. Like so many of you, I have always been a helper, and my life experiences prepared me well for serving support givers—adult children of the elderly, wives of depressed husbands, parents of troubled teens, among others. My desire is to help healthy caregivers, whose lives are surrounded by pain and dysfunction, find purpose, passion, and maybe even joy.

It's a noble cause and, I was told, a great niche. As I learned to use the powerful coaching tools being demonstrated in my professional training, I clearly understood the differences between coaching and counseling. Counseling looks at the past, coaching looks ahead. Counseling seeks healing for dysfunction, coaching is about healthy growth. Counseling focuses on relief from pain, coaching focuses on the pursuit of passion. The distinctions are all too clear. I understand them. But do those I coach understand these differences?

Each time I meet with a new client, I begin with the all important here-is-how-coaching-differs-from-counseling conversation. Knowing that most of my clients walk through very tough life situations, I explain that I will refer them to a counselor if we discover they are in an unhealthy place, can't forgive, or can't move past their circumstances. And I do.

Often I feel as though I'm walking a very fine line, like I'm balancing atop a narrow fence. On one side is the world of coaching—discovering purpose, setting goals, uncovering passions, developing gifts. On the other side of the fence is the world of counseling—dealing with the pain or getting past the anger.

If I could just stay on the coaching side of the fence, everything would be perfect. But my clients' real-life needs often position me atop the fence where I'm teetering on the edge. I cannot go to the counseling side. I must walk the fence—the fine line—and not let even my little toe slip over the edge lest I tumble into the world of counseling. It's quite a dance.

Have you been there? Any life coach walking alongside people in difficult life situations will, at some time, need to ask the question, "Should this client be working with a coach? Is it time to refer him to a counselor?"

So, how do we walk that fence? How do we, with all the integrity and honesty that a business dedicated to the glory of God deserves, give 100 percent to our clients without crossing the fine line?

Coaching the Coach Tip

There is no simple answer to that question. There are, however, some important things those of us dancing on the fence need to remember, and do, every time we coach clients who may be walking their own fine line between emotional wholeness and brokenness.

Here are four things I have found to be essential:

1. Pray Without Ceasing

As Christian coaches, we often pray for our clients. But when our clients are in extremely difficult life circumstances, prayer is not just a should-do or a nice-to-do, it is vital. Pray before every coaching session. Pray for your clients. Ask if you can pray with them. Pray that you have the discernment to know if or when clients need to transition to counseling. Pray that they are willing and able to make that transition if it becomes necessary. And pray that nothing in you will get in the way of doing what is best for your clients.

2. Talk Often about Counseling

When I coach someone who lives in the midst of turmoil, I weave the topic of counseling into almost every coaching session. When the clients' problems get in the way of our work toward their stated goals, I have to remind them of the purpose and benefit of coaching, and the fact that coaching is not a replacement for therapy. We talk frequently about the way they are responding to their circumstances, and I ask questions that help them think about and consider whether they should seek counseling. It may almost seem that I'm trying to lose clients, but unless they know the difference between coaching and counseling and seek help from the right professional at the right time, their lives won't change and our work will fail.

3. Develop Referral Relationships with Counselors

Inevitably, some of our clients living with difficult life circumstances will need to transition to a counselor. And, of course, there will be times when you see potential clients who simply will not make good coaching candidates until they seek counseling and healing for their emotional wounds. When those times come, it's important to help them find a good Christian counselor.

I first recommend that they ask if their local church has a counseling referral network. I also suggest they seek out referrals from great Christian organizations like Focus on the Family or the American Association of Christian Counselors. When your clients are local, a valuable option is referring them to someone you know personally, someone whose Christian walk is strong and who you trust professionally. Developing good referral relationships with counselors will allow you to serve your clients better and may bring you referrals when coaching is indicated.

4. Clearly Hold your Clients' Goals in Front of Them

The craziness of life's circumstances and the schemes of our enemy can often push our clients into emotional chaos. In our dance on the fine line between coaching and counseling, it is absolutely critical that we help keep our clients focused on their goals. Our powerful questions can guide them back to their stated agenda or encourage them to verbalize a new one. Our questions and coaching orientation will always be looking ahead, always pointing to the future, always helping them look at the possibilities. Our job is to help them keep their focus not on what's wrong but on what is right and on the plans God has for them.

These essentials are what Christian life coaching is all about. As we navigate that fine line, let's hold fast to the purpose and passion we so strongly believe in—the power of living life intentionally, the joy of seeing people grow and change and succeed, no matter their life circumstances.

Chapter 12

Being a Specialty Coach

As the field of coaching continues to grow, coaches often specialize in specific areas to distinguish themselves from other life coaches. Whether you choose to be a career coach, executive coach, marriage or relationship coach, or marketing coach, consider the areas in which you have experience, passion, and expertise. Also consider what segments of the population are struggling and have a real need for coaching. Stepfamilies and those who are single again are two demographic groups that can benefit from coaching.

Don't worry if you can't identify a specific area. I coached women, singles, and communicators for several years before I realized how passionate I was about coaching the coach. One day as I reflected on the number of my clients who were coaches, I realized this was a niche that I had not identified. Now, years later, coaching the coach continues to be a specialty area that gives me a real sense of meaning and fulfillment.

Coaching Stepfamilies
Dr. Evelyn de Villiers

You are the light of the world. A city on a hill cannot be hidden.
Neither do people light a lamp and put it under a bowl. Instead
they put it on its stand, and it gives light to everyone in the house.
In the same way, let your light shine before men, that they may
see your good deeds and praise your Father in heaven.
Matthew 5:14-16

A remarried couple called me for help. They heard from a friend that I not only coached stepfamilies and had written my dissertation on the subject, but also I was a mom and stepmother to seven children. They both said they were madly in love and had recently married, vowing that this time around it was going to be different. Their hope and enthusiasm, however, was beginning to unravel. Their new marriage was complicated by the children they each brought into the picture. He had three and she had two—all between the ages of eight and fifteen.

When they married, they knew they would have some challenges, but reality was harder than they'd imagined. An overwhelming sense of frustration and tension was settling into their new stepfamily. They both felt uncertain about what their roles were as stepparents, and some of the children were not adjusting well. I explained to them that it is not unusual, particularly for stepfamilies early on, to feel that the problems they may encounter are too big to handle alone. They often need help, and an experienced coach can be just what is needed to help their new family.

At the heart of the problem for this couple was that the children were not enamored with their new home life or their new stepparent, and the children's unhappiness was creating tension in the house and beginning to create problems between the couple. Some of the children were acting out, breaking the rules, and lashing out at each other and at their stepparent. The couple felt angry but also guilty that they didn't feel instant love for their stepchildren. When one spouse complained about their partner's child or imposed discipline, it not only made matters worse with the children but also created tension and anger between them as a couple.

We focused on three main tasks that would help the family move forward with greater peace and unity:

- behave toward their stepchildren as though entrusted with a children's ministry and only the biological parent would discipline each child,

- create new family rituals to promote family cohesion, and

- nurture their relationship by making time to be alone as a couple.

The sad truth is that second marriages break up more often than first marriages. This is tragic for children who have already suffered loss from their parents' first divorce. This loss is often the very reason children act out toward their new stepparent or step-siblings.

It's vitally important that a stepparent understand what they are getting into when it comes to being in the life of a child who is not biologically their own. When stepchildren act out toward stepparents, it's usually more about the child's own feelings of loss and the anxiety that change causes than it is about the stepparents' attitudes and actions.

If the stepparents view their relationship with their stepchildren more as a ministry, a responsibility, and an opportunity that honors God, then it will feel less like a chore or a burden. It is a beautiful opportunity to love in a Christlike way that is not about self but about others. What a gift it can be when a stepparent gets the opportunity in the life of a child to exemplify patience, kindness, forgiveness, grace, mercy, and love, especially when it's hard. That's why I asked this couple to leave the discipline to the biological parent.

As part of their new ministry, the stepparent was to devote time and attention to each stepchild on a daily or weekly basis to build a relationship of trust and caring. The stepparent was to find something that was important to each child and to become involved somehow so that a connection could begin to take place. Time and attention gives an underlying message to children that they are important.

For example, the stepfather took his stepson to his favorite professional baseball team's home game, and baseball became a fun and enthusiastic connection between them. The stepmother took her stepdaughter shopping for a special dress for an upcoming school dance. Afterwards, they went to lunch and just had fun. There are many creative ways to devote time and attention in the life of a child.

As an added piece of information, the couple understood that they were not replacing the child's other biological parent but were adding to the child's life as another adult who cared for them.

Children can feel cared for and adjust better to their new family structure when the parents implement traditions and shared-family rituals. These traditions and rituals can shape a family's identity and help children form shared memories with their new family unit.

I mentioned to this couple that one of the first things that I did as a new stepmom was to create photo albums for each child. These albums contained happy and funny pictures from our family vacations and special events. Every year I added new pictures to their albums. Our children are grown now, but for years when they would bring a new friend over, they would pull out their own album for a show and tell. I also took family pictures, which I framed and put up around the house. Viewing lots of family photos of us happily doing things together promoted family cohesion and happy memories.

My husband and I also made it easy on the children during holidays by being flexible about Thanksgiving, birthdays, and Christmas. Children can become anxious if their biological parents are fighting over holidays. We tried to keep the holidays consistent and predictable, but if a wrench was thrown into our plans, we tried to make it as easy as possible on the children by not overreacting and by being flexible.

I encouraged this couple to come up with their own special family rituals and traditions and involve their children in the planning. Shared rituals can help create cohesiveness and a sense of family. I also warned them that everyone might resent forced activities, which can be destructive to the relationships they were building.

A sense of family promotes feelings of security for children and parents, but you can't make your family work if you don't make your marriage work. Raising children in a stepfamily can feel like chaos at times. Finding time to be alone and nurturing the marital relationship is mandatory and will make raising children and stepchildren easier if each spouse feels supported by, loved by, and important to the other. It is also a great role model for children to see a happy, loving couple spending time together. I explained to this couple a few ideas of what they can do to nurture their relationship:

- Find time daily to talk with each other in conversations that have nothing to do with children. Talking on the phone for a few minutes or sitting down for a few minutes after work or before bed can become the best part of the day.

- Go for a walk and get out of the house. My husband and I walked on the beach nearly every day, and it was something we looked forward to.

- Plan a getaway when the children are with their other parent(s).

- Help the children understand the importance of your alone time together without interruptions.

- Show affection in front of the children, like holding hands, supporting each other's views, and treating each other with respect and importance.

- Pray together or read a daily devotional together. Focusing on God's will and God's ways is a priceless gift and often the glue needed in a stepfamily.

When a couple feels good about their relationship, everything else seems to fit into place and they'll feel like better parents as well.

No one says it is easy. Those in stepfamilies must overcome a lot of pain, grief, and loss from the past. This is especially true for the children involved.

Coaching this couple and many other stepfamilies is also a ministry of sorts. Divorce is so prevalent in America and families are breaking apart so often, even among the Christian population, that today stepfamilies are now the most common basic unit in American society. Coaching stepfamilies can provide a road map, educational resources, and a godly perspective so that more American stepfamilies have a better chance at success.

Coaching the Coach Tip

The U.S. Census Bureau provides stepfamily statistics: By 2010, stepfamilies were predicted to be more common than the conventional (two biological parents and children) or single-parent households. Now in 2013, stepfamilies are the most common form of the American family. Nearly ten million children under age eighteen are part of stepfamilies, and more than 1,000 new stepfamilies are formed each day. Sadly, second marriages break up more often than first marriages (60 percent, compared to just less than 50 percent, respectively). Second marriages with children break up even more often.

Coaching these families to manage realistic expectations, nurture the marriage, develop appropriate step parenting roles, and find fulfillment in honoring God in the lives of children is a real opportunity for each client's own personal growth and for preventing another family breakup. Coaching them is teaching, among other things, about love of the highest order. Coaching Christians to succeed in a stepfamily is bringing light to an otherwise dark place.

Coaching the Single-Again Christian
Elizabeth Gaston Cunningham

The LORD will guide you always; he will satisfy your needs in a sun-scorched land and will strengthen your frame. You will be like a well-watered garden, like a spring whose waters never fail.
Isaiah 58:11

After her divorce, it took six years and three recovery groups for Sidney to feel ready to date again. She'd been married for twenty-one years to her high-school sweetheart. Now, at the age of forty-six, she was trying online dating. The experience was both exhilarating and terrifying, she confided. It was exhilarating because of her ardent hope for new love. It was terrifying because the other women on the online dating websites somehow seemed "more attractive, more confident, more with-it."

After numerous coffee meetups and dates with men from the sites, Sidney was exhausted and uncertain. "It's like a part-time job," she lamented. "Each night, I sift through online profiles, winks, likes, pokes, requests, voice mails, texts, and emails. Then there's the sexual component. I've had a few dates with Justin, a wonderful man from my singles group. I like him a lot, but last weekend he suggested the two of us go on an overnight camping trip. I don't know what to expect—or if I can truly trust him."

Through our coaching relationship, Sidney sought to clarify goals, identify expectations, and establish boundaries that would guide her as she ventured back into the brave new world of dating.

I suggested Sidney make a list of character traits that she considered important in a potential mate—a list of "must haves" and "can't stands" that she would not be willing to compromise. Sidney enjoyed the assignment and came back the next week with a well-considered list, which we discussed item by item. This exercise also provided her with objective criteria she could use to evaluate her relationship with Justin. While she hadn't given it much thought before, Sidney now realized that his habit of dealing impatiently with service staff at restaurants and shops was a concern of hers, which she needed to stop ignoring.

To help Sidney gain more self-awareness, I asked a colleague to administer the Myers-Briggs and Enneagram personality-preference assessments, and then meet by phone with Sidney and me to review results. Sidney was intrigued by these two new lenses through which she could interpret her temperament. The tools also helped her pinpoint significant differences between Justin and herself. This led to discussions about what often draws men and women together initially (differences) versus what tends to bond them long term (similarities).

Though intellectually she grasped the concept of moral purity, Sidney confided she struggled with the notion that two middle-age adults, both sexually active during decades of marriage, would need to wait until after marriage to resume sexual activity. This led to a number of conversations exploring the meaning of love from God's perspective.

I noted that many singles approach love backwards. That is, they become involved romantically and physically and then, sometimes, they develop a deep, meaningful friendship. In even rarer cases, the relationship progresses to true, unconditional love, which seeks the highest and best for the other person.

"God's progression for relationships is just the opposite," I said. "We are to begin with what the Bible calls agape love—seeking the highest and best not only with those we date but with everyone in our lives, and then, as the Lord leads, progress to a deepening friendship while preserving the deeply sexual expressions of love for after marriage. Besides honoring God, this progression helps couples maintain their objectivity and hear from the Holy Spirit as they seek His guidance for their future."

I suggested Sidney read June Hunt's book *Biblical Counseling Keys on Dating*, which addresses this progression, and many other helpful topics, in more depth. We also explored the body-soul connection, which God hardwired into sex, as Sidney read *Sex and the Soul of a Woman* by Paula Rinehart. Guided by this book, she and I discussed the profound emotional and spiritual impact sexual intimacy has on women, in particular, and why sex outside of marriage, regardless of one's age, can be deeply damaging.

Sidney confided that her physical relationship with Justin already was progressing much faster than their friendship. She also realized she was paying little attention to seeking God's highest and best for the men she was dating.

In the weeks to come, Sidney and I enjoyed many stimulating discussions about the proper focus of dating, namely "not a rabid hunt for Mr. Right, but an earnest quest to become the person God designed us to be." In the process, I drew out a deeply held fear that Sidney was not even aware she had: the fear that, if she were to remain single, her deepest needs may never be met.

"The truth is, God has promised to meet all of your needs," I assured her. "He may choose to meet them through a husband. But even if He doesn't, you can count on His promises to meet your deepest needs for love, security, and significance." I referred her to Lawrence Crabb's book *Understanding People: Deep Longings for Relationship*. I reminded her of what God's Word says: "The Lord will guide you always; he will satisfy your needs in a sun-scorched land and will strengthen your frame. You will be like a well-watered garden, like a spring whose waters never fail" (Isaiah 58:11).

Safe People: How to Find Relationships That Are Good for You and Avoid Those That Aren't by Drs. Henry Cloud and John Townsend helped Sidney learn how to identify, and be, a safe person—one who is capable of entering into healthy relationships. Another excellent book by Cloud and Townsend, *Boundaries in Dating,* addressed many of her remaining questions about what is, and isn't, appropriate in Christian dating relationships.

After a weekend-long "silent retreat" to focus on hearing from God, Sidney decided to take a break from dating altogether, including her relationship with Justin, in order to recalibrate. "The ground we covered during our coaching sessions has given me the tools I need to approach dating with a fresh perspective," she said. "I have new confidence that, regardless of whether a new husband comes my way, I can trust God to be my hope and my future. And for me, that is enough."

Coaching the Coach Tip

Today's media-based culture provides unprecedented opportunity for, and pressure on, Christian singles reentering the world of dating. Helping them clarify goals, identify expectations, and establish boundaries can provide invaluable support during their journey. If you have experience in that area, consider making it a coaching specialty.

Planting Seeds for God
Diane Cunningham

This is my life work: helping people understand and
respond to this Message. It came as a sheer gift to me, a
real surprise, God handling all the details. When it came
to presenting the Message to people who had no background
in God's way, I was the least qualified of any of the
available Christians. God saw to it that I was
equipped, but you can be sure that it had nothing
to do with my natural abilities.
Ephesians 3:7-8 THE MESSAGE

In my professional journey, I have experienced the joy and the challenge of re-creating myself over and over again. I began my career as a counselor and later became a Life Purpose Coach. My recent metamorphosis allowed me to become the founder and president of the National Association of Christian Women Entrepreneurs. Along the way, to my delight and surprise, I found out that I had a gift for marketing.

I have no official training in marketing. I did not take one single business class in college or in graduate school. My coach training program had a few small modules on marketing. Much of what I know now I learned by watching, doing, reading, and asking. I am a risk-taking front-runner and action-type of gal who is willing to try the new gadget, gizmo, or techie tool.

The most important thing I have learned is that marketing is really about planting seeds. I see it as planting seeds for God to showcase the gift He has given me, which is a business that offers coaching and training. If I do not share, then I am not using His precious gift.

As a result of my marketing mindset, clients began to seek me for advice, training, and social media knowledge. They wanted me to show them how I had done it and to teach them how to market. I also began to coach other coaches on how to market themselves.

I found so many of my clients were being challenged in their thinking process and mindset. They felt uncomfortable promoting themselves. They also had questions about how to set prices and what to do when people asked them to volunteer their services.

As a Christian coach, I also struggled in these areas. For many years, I felt the need to work for free because in my former career one of my counseling clients took his own life and I was named in a lawsuit related to his death. After three years of legal challenges, my counseling license was suspended. I felt lost, purposeless.

I wandered, prayed, applied for sixty real jobs. Nothing happened. Finally, the clarity came. I was going to hire myself. I became an entrepreneur. God was my CEO, and I was going to be a coach.

I found a book on purpose and life coaching. This book changed my life as I began training to become a Life Purpose Coach. I was intimately aware of the deep pain of having no purpose. I had worn those shoes, and I understood the heart cry and longing for significance. The joy of coaching is that we often end up coaching from our own journey because we can help someone see the path that we have walked and get them across the bridge.

Becoming a coach wasn't easy. Many years I made just enough money to get by. I persevered. I dove into learning, training, reading, and gleaning all of the information that I could. My penchant for moving fast served me well as I forged ahead trying new things.

Eventually, women who were seeking purpose began coming to me for help as they started their own business ventures. Some of those business ventures included women who wanted to start or expand their own coaching businesses. Just the act of speaking with another person about marketing or other ideas can spark creativity. One client, Rhoda Baty from Hopeful Heart Coaching, said, "After talking with Diane I always feel like my brain is on steroids; it is going so fast generating even more ideas from her ideas."

My desire and life mission is to help every woman that I can to succeed with the God-given business in front of her. That might be a million-dollar company or a few ideas written on a napkin.

As a coach and an entrepreneur, I've learned, above all else, to trust that God has a plan for you and for your business. Get busy doing what God has called you to do; don't wait on the sidelines for everything to line up perfectly. Things will never be perfect. Start where you are with what you have. Be willing to fail. Yes, you will be failing a lot. You will also have many successes, but you have to know you will also have failures. The faster I fail, the sooner I know I will get to the next success. Allow God to show you the way. He knows much better than we do.

Coaching the Coach Tip

I believe the success in our coaching, marketing, and building our businesses is based on three interrelated actions: connect, create, and collaborate. If you are a woman looking for support, consider joining the National Association of Christian Women Entrepreneurs, which I formed in 2010.

I encourage everyone I coach to act fast now, to be brave, and to chase their dreams while supporting others and trusting the process to God's leadership. That's what connecting, creating, and collaborating is all about.

Connect

Both male and female coaches must connect with clients, prospects, vendors, trainers, mentors, colleagues, and more. We cannot do it alone. We need each other.

Create

We must be willing to open up our creative minds and spirits to new ideas, new ways of doing things, and new programs we can offer. We can allow our inner artist to emerge as we paint a new canvas. Remove the rules and regulations. Experiment. Trust the process.

Collaborate

We must work together and support one another. We must be willing to share our ideas, form a team, get a partner and lead a group, and mentor others. We cannot afford to live with a scarcity or hoarder mindset. There is plenty to go around, and we have to be willing to find our unique niche, our God-given sweet spot.

Following Your Unique Passions
Shannon Ethridge

If you wake me each morning with the sound of your loving voice,
I'll go to sleep each night trusting in you. Point out the road
I must travel; I'm all ears, all eyes before you.
Psalm 143:8 THE MESSAGE

After six months of group and individual therapy for my sex and love addiction issues, I felt like a "Girl on Fire!" My counselor actually kicked me out of her office in 1996, saying, "Okay, enough. You're healed. Now go share what you've learned with other women."

At first I thought, Whoa, I didn't sign up for that, but I soon realized that it would be a crying shame to waste my experience on just myself. I began searching for universities where I could study counseling.

One advisor asked, "What type of counseling interests you?"

"I want to help women overcome sexual compulsions," I said.

Silence. Then...a chuckle. He was laughing at my career goal. "If you limit your counseling to that degree," he stated bluntly, "you'll starve."

I considered broadening my scope but found such ponderings useless. If I wasn't helping women or couples overcome sexual or relational challenges, I just didn't feel any passion for it. To think of talking with a client for an entire hour about anything else felt like a huge hole in my bucket.

Trust your gut, Shannon. These are the words I heard God speaking as I continued praying and exploring my options. There are lots of other women like you out there. No temptation seizes you but what is common. Follow your passion.

I began working on a master's degree in counseling at Liberty University and soon developed my first manuscript on this topic I was so passionate about. I submitted it to thirteen publishers and received thirteen rejection letters. "Sexual integrity is a man's issue," they claimed. "Such a book for women will never sell."

Fortunately, Stephen Arterburn and Fred Stoeker knew better. After the *Every Man's Battle* series hit the top of the bestseller list, they began searching for someone to write a female companion series. My manuscript just happened to be sitting on their agent's desk already. It was a match made in heaven.

I was so thankful I had trusted my gut or, rather, trusted the God within my gut. After the series sold more than one million copies, I was tempted to call that college advisor and declare, "I'm not starving." (But I resisted.)

The success of the *Every Woman's Battle* series brought both blessings and challenges. I began speaking much more frequently. After events, people would email me, asking to talk with me personally. I was afraid that if I gave them an ounce of my time, they'd take a pound. My personal life coach, Dwight Bain, advised, "Folks are always going to line up for free fish and chips when they are hungry. You need to establish a system for making it a win-win relationship or else you'll burn out."

By becoming a certified life coach myself, I was able to weed out those who just wanted free advice and would drain me dry if I let them. I focused my time and energy on those who were truly dedicated to their own recovery process and on those willing to invest in a professional relationship where we work together to overcome their dysfunctional relational patterns. In exchange, they compensate me appropriately for my investment of time and expertise into their lives. Win-win.

Rather than having a hole in my bucket, my cup overflows. Whether it's a single woman trying to prepare for a healthier relationship next time around, or a married couple trying to figure out how to get back on the same sexual page, or parents trying to help their teenager navigate the waters toward sexual maturity, focusing my writing, speaking, and coaching efforts exclusively on healthy sexuality is the best career decision I ever made.

Specializing in one area of coaching rather than being a generic coach can make all the difference in how much energy you bring to the table, and how much response you receive in the way of clients. Specializing allows you to be seen as an expert in your field (or in my case, a "sexpert"). It allows you to collect specific types of fodder, which can prove quite fruitful in your speaking and writing. For example, my most recent book, *The Fantasy Fallacy: Exposing the Deeper Meaning Behind Sexual Thoughts*, is jam-packed with case studies supporting my theory that sexual fantasies are often the brain's way of trying to heal itself from past trauma. Had I not been coaching so many clients who were bewildered by their own sexual fantasies, I'm not sure I'd have caught the vision to write that book.

Maybe you're passionate about more than one type of coaching and don't want to limit yourself to one area or another. Consider how your passions might fit together, and perhaps offer both, either collectively or separately.

For example, as I travel and speak, I repeatedly get the same two types of questions. People ask a sexual question, or they ask, "How can I do what you do?" They don't always mean becoming a "sexpert." Rather, they mean creating a writing or speaking platform such that they can effectively share whatever special message God has laid on their hearts.

For years, I merely replied, "Keep plugging away," and said a prayer for God to open doors. I eventually realized there was so much more I could offer. God had allowed me some incredibly blessed opportunities, and it would be a shame to waste all of those experiences on just me. I'd worked closely with multiple marketing geniuses. I'd been personally coached by professional media trainers in Hollywood and New York. I'd been interviewed by just about every Christian television or radio program in existence and contributed to hundreds of magazines. Because God had been so good to me, I wanted to pay it forward.

So in 2009, we launched a one-year online mentorship program called B.L.A.S.T. (Building Leaders, Authors, Speakers & Teachers) and began offering small groups and one-on-one coaching to aspiring writers and speakers from all over the world. Once again, because this is an exciting, challenging road that I've personally traveled, cheering others on as they travel a similar path isn't draining at all. It's actually become one of my greatest joys.

Following a God-given passion is always energizing, eternally rewarding, and incredibly fulfilling. So if you're looking for direction, look no further than your own gut.

Coaching the Coach Tip

List your top five passions, things that really energize you as you talk about them. Perhaps it's nutrition, exercise, financial management, relationships, leadership, success strategies, or something else entirely.

Now ask yourself these questions:

- Are any of these passions such a felt need in others that many would seek professional coaching to accomplish such goals?

- Would I have more or less energy for my coaching practice if I focused exclusively on one or more of these passions?

- How would it benefit my clients for me to specialize in such a way?

- How would it benefit me personally?

Chapter 13

Growing Your Coaching Business

In this chapter, experienced coaches share different ways that you can expand your coaching business. For example, did you ever consider that instead of doing more, you could grow your business by doing less and staying focused only on God's best?

Building relationships with potential clients is the key to growth, because people first want to know you care and that they can relate to you as a person. One of the ways you can meet potential clients is by speaking at events and sharing your expertise. This not only saves you hundreds of marketing dollars but gives you visibility as a coach in your community.

Eventually, as your business grows, you'll want to gather a team of people to help you become more effective and productive. Put together a team to do the tasks you don't have the time, the knowledge, or the desire to do. For example, you may hire a professional to assist you in creating a website or page on a social media site, enabling you to connect with potential clients on the Internet. An active, professional-looking presence on the Internet where your potential clients gather will reap rewards for your coaching business.

Growing Your Business by Doing Less
Christopher McCluskey

*Why spend money on what is not bread, and your labor on
what does not satisfy? Listen, listen to me, and eat what is good,
and your soul will delight in the richest of fare.*
Isaiah 55:2

As a young man visiting a friend in the Twin Cities, I had driven out to see the original house used in The Mary Tyler Moore Show television series. I stood admiring the classic, multi-million-dollar home, a stunning Queen Anne Victorian built in 1892.

"Man, what do you do to live in a house like that?" I wondered aloud.

"I have no idea," my friend replied, "but I read that the guy who bought it didn't even know who Mary Tyler Moore was. He'd never heard of the show."

I was taken aback. "How do you live in America in the 1970s and never watch the The Mary Tyler Moore Show?"

Even as the words were leaving my mouth, I realized I'd found a piece of the answer to my original question: Part of what you do is what you don't do.

People able to buy a house like that don't spend a lot of time watching television. Their values prompt them to spend their time differently.

The insight reminded me of a similar experience back in high school. Several of us had popped into McDonald's for lunch, and I was standing in line with a wealthy buddy who'd driven me there. (His father was a third-generation business owner, and my friend already owned a convertible MGB, a TR-7, and a baby-blue vintage El Camino.)

"So, what's good here?" He asked.

I laughed at his snarky teenager sarcasm.

He looked at me and said, "Seriously, what do you usually get? I've never eaten here before."

"You've got to be kidding!" I replied. "Doesn't your family eat out?"

"Sure. Just not at McDonald's."

He was completely serious, and he wasn't being a snob.

I stared at him, wondering, How do you live in America and never eat at a McDonald's?

Same answer. I had unwittingly hit on a clue to his family's business success. Their values resulted in their viewing meals differently than most of us, which hints at many other things they did differently.

Part of what successful people do is what they don't do.

Author Stephen Covey crystallizes the lesson this way: "The enemy of the 'best' is often the 'good.'"

Not the bad, the wrong, the evil, the sinful. The good. Good things, which, because they consume our time or attention or energy or money, can rob us of the best.

Growing a coaching business for the glory of God will demand many things of you. The things you say no to will become just as important as those to which you say yes.

"Good" things that rob us of time and energy and attention for the "best" are different for everyone. For some, social events or committees they've served on for years will need to be handed over to someone else. For others, the choir or praise band or a ministry will have to be given up. For some, it's just letting go of recreational shopping. Certainly for many, it's curbing gaming or Facebooking or Web surfing or channel chasing.

Notice that none of these are inherently bad. We're not talking about addictions or secret sins that clearly need to go.

They may, in fact, be things that qualified as "best" during a previous season of life, but that season has simply passed. They continue to be good, but no longer best.

Some of you will reprioritize your love of collecting or decorating or antiquing or travel. Some will downsize your homes and forgo new cars. Some will skip a vacation, cut back on golf, get a simpler hairstyle, or give up concerts and movies. (Some will even cut back on Starbucks!)

I grew up near Cleveland, following the Browns and the Indians and the Cavaliers on television and in print, attending games, collecting ball cards, and swapping statistics with my friends.

Since starting my first business, I haven't watched a Super Bowl or a World Series or a championship game in more than twenty years. That's not a prideful statement (and it's truly not a sad statement)—it's a values statement.

As much as I would still enjoy those games, and would do nothing wrong by watching them, I find that the time and attention they require robs me of other things I now value more.

Of course, friends sometimes ask, "How do you live in America and not know who's in the Super Bowl or World Series or NBA Championship?"

You now know the answer. The very things I don't do enable me to do all that I do.

My answer will become your answer as well when people question why you've stepped down, backed off, flaked out, let go, or moved on.

As a man or woman working to establish a successful business, you are doing what very few people ever seriously attempt (although many dream of it). Fewer than nine percent of Americans are self-employed.

News flash: You're not normal. In fact, you're way out of the norm.

Ninety-one percent of adults have chosen a different path than the one you're going down. You'll have to do things differently to succeed in a career that's so different from theirs.

If you're shaken by that awareness, that's a good thing. If you're not a little fearful about starting your own business, you're not in touch with the reality of it. But that kind of fear is part of discernment—awareness of danger—and it's key to exercising wisdom and prudence and sound judgment in your venture.

Be sure that your fear is more than offset by the excitement and assurance you feel about the rightness of your decision. If it's not, turn back now and wait before the Lord until you're confident of His path.

Coaching the Coach Tip

The Christian life is nothing if not an adventure; and entrepreneurism—if that's what God has called you to—is a wild and wonderful adventure. It will stretch you in ways you've never been tested before (just like marriage and parenting and all good adventures do).

All that stretching means you'll need time and attention and energy and money—the very things so easily spent on other good things, thereby robbing you of this best.

I believe the popular saying is true: Less is more.

Use discernment in determining the best of what God is calling you to, and then start letting go of all the good things you'll no longer do.

Grow your business by doing less.

First Build a Relationship
Georgia Shaffer

*Whether you realize it or not, relationships are the fuel
that feeds the success of your business.*
Darren Dahl

While the need for coaching continues to rise, how do you connect with potential clients who want to grow personally or improve their relationships? And how do you reach those seeking guidance?

I discovered early in my career that to gain coaching clients I first had to cultivate relationships. Whether people became acquainted with me through my writing, speaking, networking, or video teaching, I realized that what I knew wasn't as important to them as whether or not they felt we had a connection. Comments from new clients, such as, "I feel like I already know you," helped me realize that before someone chooses to work with me, they want to know they can relate to me.

You can move from having no relationship to being an acquaintance to becoming their paid coach in many ways. For instance, I gained a number of clients through my video teaching on the YouTube channel. You might connect with potential clients through a blog, Facebook, or Twitter. Pick a venue that fits your personality and skill set. For others, seeing you, hearing you, and reading what you write provide glimpses into who you are as a person and a coach.

One action step you can take to grow your business is to create or fine-tune a biweekly or monthly newsletter. Recently, I attended two conferences on opposite sides of the country. In this age of blogging, the presenters at both events touted email newsletters as still being an important tool. I found that information especially interesting because I had been wondering if my email newsletter was as outdated as a cassette tape.

A newsletter is one of the top ways to engage with others because it provides

- a way to consistently engage with potential clients,
- an opportunity to repeatedly affirm the value you have to offer as a coach, and
- a tool to evaluate what's working and what isn't.

What do you put in your newsletter if you want to move people from being an acquaintance to a client? Darren Rowse, a professional blogger, speaker, and consultant, finds that he best connects when he inspires, informs, and interacts with others. These three are also important to coaches.

Inspire

Because we first process sensory stimulation through the emotional part of our brain, people are drawn to you when they emotionally connect to you. Reading or hearing your stories, especially when you are vulnerable and honest, can motivate potential clients to want to make real changes in their relationships.

People also become emotionally engaged through images and photographs. Include poignant, descriptive, or beautiful photos that will inspire your readers.

Inform

What do you know that will help others? Communicating the message that you want to provide information that will help others reach their potential is a lot different than saying you want their money. People are intuitive. Don't underestimate their ability to determine your real motive. You want to be identified as a competent coach who wants to use your expertise to help others grow. That is the type of coach about which someone will say, "I'm willing to pay for their services."

What practical articles can you write? Think about relational topics that would not only help readers but would be something they would want to share with their friends, coworkers, or family. For example, as a relationship coach I share three techniques for helping people handle the resistance that comes with change. Whether it is their spouse, a coworker, or a close friend going through a difficult transition, they can connect with someone in a meaningful way by doing the following:

- Addressing, rather than ignoring, the issue

- Normalizing their feelings, and letting people know they aren't alone or crazy

- Expressing emotions, and allowing others freedom to voice their worries and fears.

Interact

With a newsletter, for example, you could send welcome letters when people sign up. In a week or so, you could email them one of your frequently requested articles. In two weeks, you could send them a link to a thought-provoking blog or article someone else has written.

By consistently engaging with your readers, they get to know you. Share your struggles and your relational frustrations, and invite others to do the same. Pick a topic, pose a question, and encourage a discussion on Facebook. Ask your readers to share what relational topics they would like to read about, and then respond to suggestions. For instance, someone might pose a question on how to handle difficult people, which you could address in one of the upcoming newsletters.

Inform and inspire your clients, but most importantly, interact and cultivate relationships. Don't sell your coaching; instead connect with people. Focus on delivering results. When you care and put people first, your business will grow.

Coaching the Coach Tip

If you want to increase the number of clients you work with, realize that developing relationships can take more than a few months. Recently, I received an email from a man who attended one of my conferences about coaching four years ago. He had been using my coaching tools, regularly visiting my website, and reading my newsletters and articles. He wanted me to know how much he appreciated what I had shared over the years. Then he said, "I'd love to work with you as my coach." In four years we had moved from having no relationship to being client and coach because I'd consistently connected with him and provided information and tips he valued, which helped him grow. [1]

---

1 Re-printed from *Christian Coaching Today*, Volume 2, Issue 2 with permission of the American Association of Christian Counselors.

Expanding Your Influence through Community Speaking
Dwight Bain

You can get anything you want, if you help enough
other people get what they want.
Zig Ziglar

One of the fastest ways to become established as a regional expert in coaching is through offering community workshops and seminars. I've spoken to hundreds of these groups through the years and have made wonderful friends, as well as experienced some remarkable opportunities by volunteering time to add value to others. Yes, I said volunteer, since you don't get paid in dollars to give a community speech. But you can be well paid in other ways. How? Through influence, connections, multiple referrals into your coaching business, opportunities to give full-fee presentations to other groups, and wider media exposure, especially on the Internet.

Still, there's another huge benefit to you—free advertising. Consider how much you would be willing to pay in advertising dollars to be featured as an expert in front of a group of decision-makers, successful businesspeople, or community leaders? I suspect a lot because of the incredible return on investment of being in front of key people who have the capacity to hire you or refer you to other people in the community who can. The best news is that you don't have to pay to be in front of these community leaders, but you do have to be strategic.

How do you find opportunities to make community presentations? Search your local newspapers under community events, do Web searches on specific topics, or ask around to see who belongs to community groups, which are always looking for effective communicators.

Here are a few important principles to keep in mind as you begin to reach out to make a positive difference while positioning yourself as an expert in coaching.

It's Not about Marketing, It's about the Message

The goal isn't to market yourself, your book, or your services. Instead, it's about the message you give to help answer people's questions, solve their problems, and give information to help make their day or week go a little better. You want to give away as much user-friendly content in your presentation as possible. If it smells like selling, it won't work. You have to really care about your audience and help make their lives work better.

If you have a book, you could use it as a door prize. If you have business cards, you can leave them in the back, or offer a special report via email in exchange for a business card or email opt-in. This rapid follow-up builds your e-list, while showing that you are a professional who believes in giving as much away as possible. In my opinion, to respect the privacy of those who trust you, your list of contacts should never be shared or rented.

Focus on Creative Topics

Create great titles to excite and interest your audience. You might try such topics as "Getting Out of a Bad Relationship," "When to Kick Your Kids Out for Good," or "How to Gain a No. 1 Ranking on Google." You want to communicate that it's going to be a fun time of learning.

I also like to use titles and subtitles that capture the right and left hemispheres of the brain, (emotional/creative vs. logical/rational). For instance, I have used "Relationship Renewal (right hemisphere title): How to Recover, Rebuild and Renew with the People You Care about Most (left hemisphere subtitle)." The subtitle is often a lengthier description of how to do what it is you have described in your main title. With titles and subtitles like these, you'll catch the attention of a much wider audience while keeping your thoughts focused on a specific topic.

Be Professional and Be Prepared

If you think you will have problems speaking publicly, hire a communication coach to help you learn the necessary skills and confidence.

At every speaking engagement, arrive early, but be flexible because frequently you may not get the full time you were allotted due to other club business that may be taken care of. The more prepared you are ahead of time, the easier you can edit on the fly to end on time. You must finish on time, no matter when you get started, because people on a tight schedule will actually get up and leave in order to stay on their schedules.

Hand-outs reinforce your message and also provide a place for you to add your contact information at the bottom of the sheet. People often keep these for years if you three-hole punch them or print on pre-drilled paper, which adds greater value to the sheet by suggesting that it's important enough to take home and put into a notebook.

If you have professional marketing material at a back table, that's great. In this communication setting, though, the main strategy is to give an amazing talk first and foremost.

Give a Great Talk and Get a Lot of Great PR

Once you are comfortable with the process and give great presentations on a regular basis, you can leverage your talks in several ways that will bring in new opportunities for taking your message to new audiences. Ask to professionally record or video tape your presentation. These recordings can be turned into a new CD, podcast, DVD, or online webinar. You can use the items as bonuses, adding greater value to your website. Or they can become stand-alone products you can add to your shopping cart of online resources. When groups from outside your area contact you about the possibility of speaking to their audiences and ask to preview one of your presentations, you can easily mail your DVD or direct them to your podcast.

Community workshops add value to everyone involved—to you, to your audience, and to those who will meet you in the future because they heard about someone who cared enough to take their message to the marketplace to share with others. Do that long enough, and you'll be the busiest professional in your region—and it all started with a free speech.

Coaching the Coach Tip

To get your thinking started, consider the following types of groups in your area that need communicators:

- Business groups such as the chamber of commerce or female executives

- Service or civic clubs like Rotary, Sertoma, Lions, or Kiwanis

- Medical groups like nurses, interns, residents, or hospital committees

- Networking groups like BNI, Focus International, or BabbleBee

- Faith-based groups like churches, ministries, or the retreats they sponsor

- Health groups, such as the American Heart Association or American Red Cross

- Political organizations or political action committees (PACs)

- Emergency services like police, fire, EMS groups, or safety committees

- Women's clubs like the Junior League, Curves, or MADD

- Athletic groups like Masters Swimming, soccer clubs, or hunting groups

- Education groups like parent teacher organizations or school volunteers

- Fraternal orders like the Elks, Eagles, Moose, or the Fraternal Order of Police

- Seniors' groups, usually found at senior centers or retirement centers

- Youth groups sponsored by churches, Youth for Christ, or Junior Achievement

- Parenting groups, especially young parents such as Mothers of Preschoolers

- Professional trade associations of which there are more than 22,000 in the United States.

Groups like these are looking for coaches like you right now to line up as the speaker at their next event.

Every Coach Needs a Team
Kathy Carlton Willis

Now all glory to God, who is able, through his mighty power at work within us, to accomplish infinitely more than we might ask or think.
Ephesians 3:20 NLT

I just can't handle this any longer!" Gina vented. "I love what I get to do as a coach, but I don't like all the other details I need to keep track of to run a business and a household. I feel tired all the time, and I know I'm not much fun to be around when I'm so stressed. I don't think my to-do list can get any longer. How do you manage to get it all done? You seem to have it all together." Gina aired her frustrations with me one on one after I spoke at a coaching seminar.

"Have you considered getting some help?" I asked. "I used to feel overwhelmed by all the duties I thought I had to deal with, and then I realized I could delegate a lot of it and fill my day doing what I love to do."

"Well, I guess I could let go of some of these things I think I have to do myself. It's hard to take my hands off some of these tasks because it feels like I'm no longer in control." Gina hung her head and sighed.

"Just remember, every coach needs a team," I reassured Gina as we walked back to our rooms.

If you have too few hours in your day to tackle your to-do list, you are in the same predicament as Gina and many other coaches—you need help. By delegating duties, your day will flow better with less stress, and you'll have time to rediscover a life outside of work. Just like hearing the siren that alerts us to an approaching first responder, help is on the way.

First responders use a list of diagnostics to decipher how best to help their patients. Here's a list of diagnostics we can use as coaches:

1. Determine how many hours a week you would like to recover. Perhaps you have something new you want to add to your life, but you can't do it until you kick something else off the to-do list. Or maybe extra work has piled up because you thought you could do it but now you are burning the candle at both ends and running out of wax. Often just ten hours a week makes a difference between feeling your project list is going to make or break you.

2. Decide exactly what you do that can be delegated to someone else. Often, the first "to go" items from your to-do list involve household chores, such as cleaning, cooking, shopping, laundry, lawn care, babysitting, and errands. Have a family meeting and decide if the chore roster can be divided differently or if you should hire household help. Family members might balk at pitching in to help until they hear how much money they can save by handling these tasks "in-house."

3. Determine which tasks related to your job can be handled by an assistant. Know exactly what it is you want an assistant to do for you before you begin the hiring process. Will the person be making phone calls, doing mailings, or following up on emails? Make a list of what you do for your coaching business that you can hand off to someone else, and use it to build a job description for your helper. Again, it's possible that others in the family will want to pitch in and help when they realize they can save the family budget a nice-sized dollar figure each month. Do not, however, hire family if they aren't equipped for the task. It's a recipe for disaster to be the boss of a family member if their giftedness and interests don't match up to the project list.

Coaching the Coach Tip

Just as Gina learned she could use her time more effectively by gathering or building a team to handle the workload in her life, you can determine the best ways to be productive, and have time left over for a life outside of coaching. When working with staff, there are several elements to keep in mind.

1. Select staff with a similar passion and work ethic. Make sure their integrity and loyalty is reliable. I select workers who are passionate in their Christian faith, because if they have an intimate relationship with the Lord, I can teach them the rest.

2. Assign tasks that match their giftedness. I've reassigned roles based on strengths and weaknesses, which ends up strengthening the entire firm and keeping staff content and challenged.

3. Communication is key, especially if you have a virtual assistant. Document instructions through email, work assignment lists, and so forth, so no tasks are missed and no one gets ruffled feathers over misunderstandings. Be specific about deadlines and priorities.

4. Be sure to have face time with your virtual assistant at least a couple of times a year so that you can rekindle the person's enthusiasm for the job. There's something about spending time together that can't be duplicated online or on the phone.

5. Look into all the tax requirements related to hiring staff. Make sure you are above reproach with quarterly withholdings, worker's compensation, and unemployment taxes and reports, if required. Or consider hiring contract or freelance staff by the project or as needed rather than by hourly or salary employment.

6. Compliment often. It's easy with the stresses of work to assume our staff members know we appreciate them. I praise them every opportunity I get and tell them specific things I like about how they do their jobs.

7. Evaluate routinely. Spell out what you want to see improved and provide the resources for that to happen. Give bonuses or gifts for jobs well done. Restructure job descriptions or numbers of hours based on the evaluation and the workload. Set goals for the future and make sure your staff knows what these goals are so that everyone is working toward the same dreams.

By forming your own team, you too can experience less stress from time demands and more opportunities to do what you do best. Whether you have volunteer helpers from your household or paid assistance through on-location or virtual staff, figure out the best way to delegate tasks. You'll trade in feelings of being overwhelmed and overworked for the ability to operate in your strengths and have time left over for a life outside of coaching. It's time to recruit your team.

Meeting Your Clients in Cyberspace
Mary Sorrentino

Tune your ears to wisdom, and concentrate on understanding.
Proverbs 2:2 NLT

Some things man was never meant to know. For everything else, there's Google.
Unknown

Phishing. Cookies. Cache. Megabytes. Cloud. Permalink. Do these words make your head spin? If so, you're not alone.

For most of the population, the world of computer technology has always been a land where nerds spoke a foreign language, discussing incomprehensible and completely uninteresting concepts. That's probably even more evident in the world of coaching than in many other professions. After all, coaching is all about relationships—real people with real goals, dreams, and desires. So it's no wonder that those of us who choose to become coaches are people people. We care far more about what goes on in people's minds and hearts than what happens on their computer screens.

But today, with the boom of Facebook, Twitter, Skype, instant messaging, and all the other social media services that even Grandma is using to connect to those she loves, it has become harder and harder to distinguish between what's happening in people's hearts and on their computers. Today, people not only get their world news electronically, they communicate with their families and friends in cyberspace as well. The world is meeting in the "cloud"—that ever mystifying place out there somewhere where all our online computing takes place. So, if everyone, including our coaching clients, are getting their information, meeting their friends, shopping, researching, and

251

even finding spouses in the mysterious world of the Internet, all of us highly relational coaches had better figure out a way to reach our clients right where they live—online.

The problem is most of us don't know how. I can't even count how many times I have heard coaches say, "I know I need an email newsletter, and a website, and a Facebook page, and, oh, yes, a Twitter account, but I have no clue where to even start." Some clients who come to me for technical coaching are still having a hard time just trying to figure out how to attach their welcome packet documents to an email message.

Yet in this new world of mobile computing and e-everything, people are on their Netbooks, Smartbooks, e-readers, tablets, smart phones, and computers more than ever before.

Coaching the Coach Tip

How do coaches, most of whom are not left-brained computer whizzes, navigate in a technology-driven marketplace to reach the people we want to serve? Here are a few tips to get you started.

1. Don't Think You Need to Know it all Before You Begin

Technology changes almost as fast as the speed of sound. Okay, so that's a slight exaggeration, but the point is that technology is changing far too fast for most of us to keep up. Even when I was in corporate information technology, my coworkers and I knew that things changed much too quickly for any one of us to know everything about everything. That should be very freeing to those of you who think you need to understand something completely before you stick your little toe in the water. Remember, you can't know it all. With the wonderful world of Google at your fingertips, all the information you need is readily available when you need it.

2. Start with the Basics

Before you dive into the cyber world of the Internet, know that your computer is well maintained and secure. Be sure you are backing up your data every day. Get one of the best security suites available to protect your computer from viruses, spam, spyware, malware, and other cyber-attacks. Run routine computer maintenance tasks regularly, like disk defragmentation and disk cleanup if you use a Windows operating system. If you are using an Apple Mac computer, depending on the version, your system still needs to be maintained and protected. Once you are sure you are protecting and maintaining your computer, you can move on to deciding how you will begin developing your Internet marketing presence.

3. Decide on One Internet Marketing Tool to Develop First

One of the biggest problems we have in the world of technology is simply overload. When we think about all we should be doing—creating and maintaining a website, an e-newsletter, a Facebook page, a LinkedIn page, Twitter, Pinterest, not to mention our basic computer security and maintenance—it becomes overwhelming and many of us simply freeze and do nothing. Start by developing an online marketing plan. Learn where your clients spend most of their time and meet them there. If you're a career coach, start with a LinkedIn page. If you're a life coach, start with a Facebook page or a website. It's important to know where your audience hangs out, so you can develop your presence where they live. Then decide either whether you have the time and technical skills to do that development yourself or if you need to hire an expert to do it for you.

4. Know Your Strengths and Weaknesses

In an effort to save money when we're starting our coaching business, many of us decide to do as much as possible ourselves, and that often includes creating and maintaining our websites, newsletters, Facebook pages, and using other technology tools. We sometimes forget that the amount of time we spend learning how to do all these things is time we could be spending on other marketing activities that may be more in line with our gifts and talents. So, if you are an ex-IT geek like me, go ahead and create, play, and develop your own online marketing presence. But if computers are not your thing, or if you simply don't enjoy trying to conquer a whole new world, then it may be much more cost-effective in the long run to hire someone to do your technical work for you.

5. Don't Abdicate Responsibility

Wait a minute. Didn't I just say you may want to hire a technical expert if computers are not your strength? Yes. But even if you decide to hire a techno-guru, it is critically important not to abdicate complete responsibility to someone else. This is your business. Nobody cares about it like you do. You need to know enough about all the aspects of your business, even technology, to wisely oversee those who work for you. As I used to say when I managed a team in corporate information technology, "I don't need to know how to do your job. I just need to know enough to be sure you know how to do it!" That's your role if you choose to hire someone else to do your technical work. Be wise. Read. Take some free or inexpensive online technology courses so you can speak the language. Google "online computer training" to see all the options available to you. Don't allow yourself to be in a position where you have to blindly trust someone else because you don't know enough to discern if they are telling you the truth. That's a dangerous place to be. We are all stewards of what God has given us. Steward your coaching business well.

Chapter 14

Feeding Your Coaching Soul

Are you taking time to nurture your soul? Are you intentionally looking at and removing junk from your heart, such as petty grudges and deep resentments? Do you have a personal stress prevention plan you use so that you are in a position to help your clients with their ongoing stress? Are you following the instruction of Proverbs and thinking on whatever is true, excellent, and praiseworthy? Do you have someone keeping you accountable so that you routinely cultivate the spiritual practices that will feed your soul? And, finally, when was the last time you unplugged and took a sabbatical? Whether you get away for a day or a week, give yourself permission to rest.

Remove Your Trash Regularly
Georgia Shaffer

Don't ask yourself if you are making a difference in the lives of others.
The question is what kind of a difference are you making?
Georgia Shaffer

Have you ever neglected to take out your garbage on collection day? Perhaps you forgot. Maybe you were just too tired, or you were out of town. Remember the result? First, an unpleasant odor develops; then, an awful stench. And then, unwanted creatures, such as gnats, flies, or maggots appear. The failure to properly dispose of our waste spawns all kinds of undesirable and unhealthy conditions.

Similarly, failure to deal with our hurts, grudges, insecurities, irritations, and resentments in a proper and timely fashion not only adversely impacts our emotional and spiritual well-being but also affects our clients.

If you want your character as a coach to be one that positively influences others, then you need to be intentional about clearing out negative attitudes, thoughts, and feelings that are weighing you down. As the writer of Hebrews suggests in chapter 12, verse 1, we want to "throw off everything that hinders and the sin that so easily entangles, and…run with perseverance the race marked out for us." It's our awareness of what's holding us back along with the commitment to take action that enables us to remove our emotional trash.

Since we all have plenty of heart-junk and only God knows everything that is in our hearts, it's essential to carve out time for prayer and self-evaluation. Are you asking God to show you what grudges or other negative thoughts and feelings you've grown accustomed to, are ignoring, or can't see? Here are a couple of questions to help you get started.

What Unfulfilled Expectations or Desires Am I Ignoring?

Ask yourself if you are ignoring any unfulfilled expectations or desires. Dreams and desires are a good thing, but sometimes our legitimate desires or unmet expectations can subtly or not so subtly become something we believe we need. We discount the negative effect they have in our personal relationships or in our work. For example, maybe you desire a calendar filled with coaching clients. Before long you may come to believe it is essential to your well-being. You become fixated on fulfilling this desire. Your thoughts, words, and actions become all-consuming to the detriment of your health and to your relationships with others. You may even become angry with God.

There is a fine line between hoping a desire will be met and expecting or demanding that it be met. Be willing to let go of your desires when they aren't fulfilled according to your time frame. Surrender what can't be met right now, or might never be met, so that you can embrace the reality of what is.

If you continue to ignore your expectations, there will come a point when you're no longer aware you're still carrying them around.

What Grudges or Resentments am I Holding Onto?

Ask yourself if you are holding grudges or resentments. The process of moving from a negative event to a grudge to full-blown resentment is subtle and gradual. Like living near a fast-food restaurant and getting used to the smell of grilled meat or spices, resentment is something we quickly grow accustomed to. We become desensitized to its existence.

One morning after reading Isaiah 43, I considered God's mercy in blotting out my sins compared to how I remembered others' transgressions against me. I realized I was holding tightly to an old grudge. Just the night before, I had shared with a friend every little detail about something someone had done to me years ago.

One simple prayer, admitting my unforgiveness and asking God to heal and restore my heart, made such a dramatic difference. I couldn't believe how light and free I felt compared to the months before. Georgia, I wondered, why did you hold onto those grudges for so long? I knew why. I had grown used to them. They had become such a part of me that I didn't notice how unattractive they were.

Ask God to shine His light in your heart and mind. You may be surprised by the things God brings to your attention. The more quickly you identify any draining thoughts and feelings, the more quickly you can work through them. Like me, you might even wonder why you held onto that grudge for so long.

Trash removal is about getting rid of anything that corrupts your character so you are free to be the person and the coach God created you to be. Be willing to take your emotional junk to the dumpster regularly. You will not only experience stronger relationships, better attitudes, and less stress, but you will also positively impact the lives of those you coach.

Coaching the Coach Tip

Because we gradually gather all kinds of discouraging thoughts and negative feelings over time, it is helpful to routinely take time for self-examination and to compare this month to last month. Which of the following statements best describes where you are today?

- My heart is becoming heavier with discouragements, doubts, and insecurities.

- My heart has some worries, fear, and anxiety.

- My heart is becoming lighter and freer.

- My heart is light, and I am free to be who God created me to be.

Be willing to see what is weighing you down and make the commitment to get rid of it. No matter how insignificant it may seem, dealing with it allows you to make a positive difference in the lives of those you coach.

Put the Mask on Yourself First
Dr. Eric Scalise

Though youths grow weary and tired,
And vigorous young men stumble badly,
Yet those who wait for the LORD
Will gain new strength;
They will mount up with wings like eagles,
They will run and not get tired,
They will walk and not become weary.
Isaiah 40:30-31 NASB

Effective life coaching often requires both a compassionate response and a certain level of emotional resilience. Merriam-Webster's dictionary defines the term compassion as a "sympathetic consciousness of others' distress, together with a desire to alleviate it." Much of the research on this subject underscores the critical importance of the helping relationship, and coaches are frequently in close proximity to the emotional suffering and resulting pain of those they work with. Herein lies both a potential problem for any coach (increased stress and burnout), as well as a wonderful opportunity (to represent God as one of His ambassadors).

The Lord gave me a wonderful life lesson a few years back while I was flying overseas to speak with more than a thousand pastors at a conference on, of all things, stress and burnout. It had been a particularly chaotic and hurried week leading up to my departure—something I'm sure many of you can readily identify with. Beyond that, making difficult connections in multiple airports due to weather conditions was not what I had in mind. When I finally boarded my last flight, I managed to grab a newspaper and was ready to slow down and relax. Soon after I sat down, the crew began their normal pre-flight announcements. If you travel frequently, as I do, you may tend to ignore the flight crew as they cover airplane rules, overhead compartments, seatbelts, emergency exits, and the like. The newspaper was much more interesting anyway.

I was perfectly content in tuning out when the voice of the flight attendant came across the loudspeaker, "Ladies and gentlemen, I know many of you have already had a long day and that you're tired, but if you would be so kind as to set aside your reading materials for a few brief moments, we would like to cover some important safety information with you."

This at least prompted me to pull the corner of the newspaper back a few inches and glance up into the aisle. To my surprise, there was a flight attendant standing just a few feet away smiling at me with "that look." Here I was going to teach on ministry-oriented stress and I was swimming in it at the moment. Of course, I put down the paper, sighed, and smiled back.

In the middle of the preflight announcements, I heard the following, which I have heard many times before but usually gloss over.

"If we should experience the sudden loss of cabin pressure, oxygen masks will deploy from the ceiling above you. If you are traveling with small children, please put the mask on yourself first and then assist the child."

The Holy Spirit immediately began to stir me regarding this profound truth. Why should parents put on their mask first? One would tend to think it would be more humane, loving, and compassionate to help the children first. Since children are probably more vulnerable and less able to take care of themselves, the most responsible course of action is for parents to make sure they are in a position to help and facilitate care. To do that, they need to be stable and breathing in the oxygen themselves.

The same is true for all of us as life coaches. When people bring their issues into a session or are in the middle of a crisis, they are typically less mobile, less resourced, more incapacitated, and anxious, and perhaps less able to discern the voice of the Lord at the moment than we are (at least in theory). If we want to ensure our availability to the Lord and to others, we must take care of ourselves first—appropriately and in a balanced way—or we risk becoming ineffective, and at times even a hindrance to what God is trying to accomplish. If we're always last, we won't always last.

Coaching the Coach Tip

So, how do we sustain joy along the way? When the unexplainable, the unpredictable, or the traumatic event takes place, theological rulebooks are often inadequate when a response of compassion is required. At times, the impact that accompanies the sheer level of emotion we are confronted with as a coach can overwhelm even the most capable and mature believers. A primary challenge for most coaches is the simple reality that self-care is something we tend to focus on when it pertains to others and not necessarily to ourselves.

Coaches are not only susceptible to increased levels of stress, but also when combined with a call to love and serve others, the result is what is commonly referred to as compassion fatigue. Compassion fatigue can be understood as a comprehensive exhaustion that takes place over time when one is constantly in the giving position and as a result, loses his or her ability and motivation to experience joy, satisfaction, or to feel and care for others. It is sometimes referred to as secondary, or vicarious, stress because it is associated with the emotional residue related to the cause of caring.

The following are a few core principles you may find helpful in creating a personal stress-prevention plan. Prayerfully develop each of these into something tailored to your needs and situations. Write the plan down and review it every week. Start by being honest with yourself and open to what the Holy Spirit is speaking.

1. Learn how to recognize the stress-producing areas in your life that might need attention, and then take ownership of what needs to be done.
2. Learn how to renew your mind and walk in God's truth.
3. Learn to rest, because the nature of God has much to do with rest.
4. Learn to be silent and learn to be still.
5. Learn to give your burdens to God each day.
6. Learn to triage your daily and life events.

7. Learn to resolve those things that can be attended to easily and quickly.
8. Learn to manage your time by saying no; otherwise, your time will control you.
9. Learn to delegate to others whenever, wherever, and however it is appropriate.
10. Learn the value of authentic relationships, and find one or two key people in your life to be accountable to.

Christian coaching is a high and sacred calling in which we humbly, yet transparently, represent Christ to a lost and hurting world. In order to "run with endurance the race that is set before us" (Hebrews 12:1 NASB), we must be deliberate when it comes to our own self-care. Only then, can we put on the compassion of Christ and consistently manifest His grace, truth, and love to all who so desperately need His touch. May you have true joy in the journey.

How Do You Want To Feel Today?
Linda Beck Johnson

*Whatever is true, whatever is noble, whatever is right, whatever
is pure, whatever is lovely, whatever is admirable—if anything
is excellent or praiseworthy—think about such things.*
Philippians 4:8

Often, the first thoughts that come to mind at the beginning of a day surge toward the things to do, things left undone, or things we feel can never be done. Clients come to us wanting change and fulfillment. Defining where we are and where we want to be comes with a payoff, usually after the process is in motion. It involves what we feel in response to the direction we take. What would happen if we moved those feelings from the end to the beginning of the process? What could we gain or lose?

Genesis 1:27 says that God created humankind in His image, in the divine image He created him; male and female He created them. If we believe we reflect the image of the Divine, then fear cannot exist. As I rest in silence, I forget about doing and I open myself to feel the feelings I want to feel for today, this year, and the rest of my life. The choice of feelings is mine. I am in control.

I've never known a person who wanted to feel powerless, incompetent, unloved, or frightened. Rather we want the best for ourselves because that is what God wants. It's how we are wired.

In John 14:1-2, Jesus says, "Do not let your hearts be troubled. You believe in God; believe also in me. My Father's house has many rooms; if that were not so, would I have told you that I am going there to prepare a place for you?"

For some of us, taking charge of feelings is a new place. What provides the motivation for us to open the door and enter this new place? I become motivated as I read and study verses about the emotions I want to have. When I consciously take charge of what

I want to think and subsequently feel, I tend to gravitate to certain passages of Scripture such as these:

- The joy Jesus speaks of in John 15:11: "I have told you this so that my joy may be in you and your joy may be complete."

- The love He speaks of in John 15:12: "My command is this: Love each other as I have loved you," and of which Jeremiah records the Lord saying in Jeremiah 31:3, "I have loved you with an everlasting love."

- The power that Jesus promises in John 14:20: "On that day you will realize that I am in my Father, and you are in me, and I am in you."

Try it for just a few moments. Close your eyes. Think about and feel the feelings you want to feel for the rest of your life. Be patient and begin to feel God's abundance.

Feelings are powerful. Several years ago, I was working with a group of women facilitating a weekend retreat, and I was asked to give a talk about grace. This was a very busy time in my life. I was working for a Fortune 200 company as an advisor to a senior vice president. My position required extensive travel and long workdays. I was also working on my master's degree in religious studies and taking a course on the Scriptures. Pressure dominated my life.

The psyche is an incredible source of goodness, however, and sometimes brings incredible surprises. For example, for my master's program I had to choose a topic in the Gospel of John for a term paper. I made my choice but was out of town the day the class assignments were approved by the instructor. The next week my professor told me I would be writing about joy in the Gospel of John. I respectfully informed him that my choice was the "I am" sayings. After protesting many times, I finally said, "Okay, joy it is," and begrudgingly began to research the topic.

At the same time, I was trying to write my talk about grace. I had given many talks before, but for some reason, this one just wasn't coming together. I decided to enlist a prayer partner. I pondered the meaning of the idea of "joyful noise" as I typed her email address. I thought about my first weekend retreat and the wonderful friendships I had made. The theme of that retreat was "The Joy of the Lord is Your Strength." A few days later, a coworker gave me *Surprised by Joy,* a book by C. S. Lewis, and a little statue titled Joy.

During the next three weeks the word "joy" inundated my life. My daily meditations had titles like "Joy-Tribute," "You Are My Joy," and "Full Joy." I began to chuckle as I envisioned a cosmic conspiracy designed to let me know I really was supposed to write a paper on joy.

The first day of the retreat came. I awakened knowing that on some level, I had not met my expectations for my talk, but dwelling on it was not the answer. I decided to just stop, close my eyes, and feel the feelings I wanted to feel. All of a sudden, I was overcome with love from these women on the retreat team. With them, I'd always felt like I had my own personal squad of cheerleaders rooting for me.

I thanked God for each one by name: "Thank you for Mary, she is so kind and always on my side. Thank you for Cookie, she is always on my side," and so on. Each time I thanked God, the response, "Jesus is on your side," would come through in my spirit, and each time more forcefully. I acknowledged these thoughts with, Yes, I know Jesus is on my side. Finally, the response took a very loud, very visual form: Jesus is On Your Side—JOYS!

I realized that I was supposed to talk about "joys" infused in the gift of unconditional, perfect love called grace. If it's grace, it's joy! And I felt both God's grace and joy as I spoke to the ladies at the retreat.

I continue to see God's reminders of what I choose to think about and the feelings that follow. Recently, when I opened my email, I found an excerpt from *The Strangest Secret: How to Live the Life You Desire* by Earl Nightingale. It was a little story about how our minds cultivate what we put into them. Like two seeds planted in fertile soil, one seed of corn and the other the seed of a poisonous plant, each will grow if we nourish it.

And so our minds work in the same way. What we tend to overlook is that we control the seeds we want to plant and we can refuse to water and feed poisonous seeds. The feelings I want to feel gently sustain and invigorate me. They help me open doors, and then close others. Most of all, these feelings enable me to help others do the same.

Coaching the Coach Tip

To generate the energy needed to take action, remember that your choices are important. Take charge of what you think by focusing on whatever is true and noble and pure. God's goodness will infuse your feelings to refresh your spirit and jump-start the creative process.

Daily Renewal for Your Coaching Soul
Dr. Sylvia Hart Frejd

Are you tired? Worn out? Burned out on religion? Come to me. Get
away with me and you'll recover your life. I'll show you how to take
a real rest. Walk with me and work with me—watch how I do it. Learn
the unforced rhythms of grace. I won't lay anything heavy or ill-fitting on you.
Keep company with me and you'll learn to live freely and lightly.
Matthew 11:28-30 THE MESSAGE

She walked into my office, sat down, and with tears in her eyes said, "I am a seventy-six-year-old woman, and I have spent most of my life languishing and distant from God. I don't know how much longer I will live, but starting today I want to spend the rest of my life daily walking with God."

She had been burned out on religion and wanted to recover her life. It was a joy to walk my client through the steps to developing her spiritual walk and to watch her grow in her love and commitment to God. When our coaching sessions ended, I saw her transformation. She was finally living freely and lightly.

The most important thing we do as coaches is to help people be daily renewed in God's presence. The reality is that as a coach I can't take people further spititually than I have gone myself. You and I have to daily experience renewal for our soul before we meet and share with our coaching clients.

Pastor Rick Warren says, "You need to get a spiritual coach. Call them a friend, a partner, a mentor, a disciple, a Timothy or Paul—or whatever. It doesn't matter what you call them. Just get a friend who says, 'I am going to hold you accountable, you're going to hold me accountable, and we're going to help each other grow.'"

268

Coaching the Coach Tip

I would like to serve as your spiritual renewal coach and walk you through seven steps to having daily spiritual renewal. I pray that these steps will help you experience daily spiritual renewal for your coaching soul and that this renewal will flow into the lives of your coaching clients.

1. Meditate on God's Word

This means that you don't just quickly read through your daily Bible reading, check the box, and consider it done. Read Scripture and absorb the words. Let them sink deep into your soul. Keep plenty of 3 x 5 cards on hand and be ready to write down a specific verse that God impresses on your heart that day. You can also laminate your Scripture cards and put them by your sink, in your children's lunches, or at your desk at work or at school. In a journal, write down the time and place you will meet daily with God in His Word and in prayer.

2. Practice Praise and Gratitude

The number one question I am asked as a life coach is this: "What is God's will for my life?" Scripture answers that question for us in 1 Thessalonians 5:18, "give thanks in all circumstances." Research in psychology tells us that thankfulness and gratitude are the healthiest emotions we can have. I try to listen to praise and worship music all day on my smart phone. Practicing praise opens up our spirit to God's presence. Take time daily to write out three things you are grateful for. As you journey through your day, be intentional in finding things to thank God for and stay in an attitude of praise.

3. Have Conversations with God

I want to coach you to be in a continual attitude of prayer, to pray all day long, to be mindful of your thinking and your self-talk, and to turn it into prayers. After all, praying is just talking to God like you would your best friend. Your goal is that praying would become as natural to you as taking your next breath. Do you have a prayer partner? If you don't have one, pray for God to send you one. I meet with my prayer partner on the phone once a week and it has been one of the greatest blessings of my life. It is such an encouragement to know that she is praying for me during my week. Write in your journal the name of your prayer partner, and specifically when you will meet.

4. Practice Confession and Self Examination

In my coaching experience, the biggest roadblock my clients face is unforgiveness. Daily forgiving others will become one of the greatest gifts you give yourself, as it will remove the roadblock that is keeping you from being all God has for you to be. God's Word tells us how we are to respond to our enemies, those who have done us wrong. We are to forgive them, love them, pray for them, bless them, and do good to them. Write in your journal the name(s) of who you need to forgive today and who you need to ask for forgiveness.

5. Surrender your All

True surrender of our lives to God is not a onetime event. It is a daily surrendering to God's will and purpose that leads to a surrendered life. Your relationship with the Lord must always have top priority over anything else. When you seek Him first every day and ask Him to help you put your life in order, He will do that. Note in your journal what God is asking you to surrender today. Next, pray and pause after each sentence of the following prayer of surrender: "Lord, renew my mind so I may know You. Lord, touch my eyes so I may see You. Lord, open my ears so I may hear You. Lord, guard my tongue so I may praise You. Lord, melt my heart so I may love You. Lord, take my hands so I may serve You. Lord, guide my feet so I may know You."

6. Cultivate Silence and Solitude

There is an epidemic in America and you probably have already been exposed to it. It's called "hurry sickness." With so much vying for our attention—smart phones, iPods, laptops, Facebook—we have lost the art of being still. If we don't take time to be still, then we can't teach others to be still. Try to practice mini-solitude retreats during your day and keep a journal of what God says to your heart. He is speaking. Are you listening?

7. Focus your Calling

Daily you must be reminded to focus your vision and seek God's plan, purpose, and goals for your life. D. L. Moody said, "The world has yet to see what God will do with and for and through and in and by the man or woman who is wholly consecrated to Him." The purposeful life is lived one purposeful day at a time. Doing what matters today will lead to God's purpose for your life. Write in your journal about what God has for you to do today.

Give Yourself a Break
Jerome Daley

What you're after is truth from the inside out.
Enter me, then; conceive a new, true life.
God, make a fresh start in me,
shape a Genesis week from the chaos of my life.
Psalm 51:6, 10, THE MESSAGE

I'm riding low in the water," she admitted. "I feel overwhelmed with all that life is throwing at me, and I know my clients aren't getting my best anymore."

Jenny was my favorite client. You know how it is—you like all your clients and feel deeply vested in the success of each. But there is always one. When you glance at your schedule for the day and see his or her name as your two o'clock, you light up. Every session with that person leaves you jazzed, energized by the mystical synergy that crackles across time and space to produce meaning and momentum.

Jenny was a coach herself, a deeply spiritual person who I admired immensely. She juggled clients, family, health challenges, church ministry, and a part-time corporate job with an energy and agility that left me breathless. But the sum of all these parts had left her drained. Shallow. Well below the thriving spiritual and emotional watermark of abundance she craved.

"What do you need, Jenny?" I asked.

"I guess I need a break," she murmured, almost apologetically.

And so Jenny spent the next month preparing for a sabbatical. With typical abandon, she practiced saying no in order to carve out some soul space. She told her clients she was taking a month off; nobody blinked. She told her boss she needed two weeks off; done. She postponed a speaking gig and began brainstorming how she would spend this time of self-care. One week at a friend's empty beach house. One week at a retreat center. Plus two weeks at home, carrying her part-time job hours but setting everything else to the side.

As Jenny and I continued our coaching sessions across that sabbatical month, I watched her soul come back to life. Like the proverbial wilted flower, a bit of water and sunshine worked its magic and set her back on the path to thrive internally, and help her clients do the same. To her credit, when it came time for reentry, she wisely chose not to pick everything back up that she had been carrying.

Does this story sound familiar? See any glimmers of yourself in Jenny? Most of us know this space and have occupied it at one time or another. Maybe repeatedly. Over the past few years, I've probably coached a dozen leaders through some sort of sabbatical, ranging from a long weekend to three months in length. Without exception, the results have been transformational. Giving ourselves a break is desperately necessary for us to go the long haul as coaches.

From my clients, as well as from my own journey, I've learned a few things about the call for the much-needed break. First, none of us are exempt from seasons of strain and weariness. Second, life doesn't play fair. Circumstances will either conspire to hit hard and suddenly from multiple sides or undermine you with slow, extended erosion. Third, the need for a sabbatical is one of God's great gifts to be embraced with gratitude. The break is a gift, and the need itself is a gift. I don't have time to unpack that here, but I'm guessing you know what I mean.

Now let's get practical. How?

Of the many things that could be said, I'll share two applications, a recurring sabbatical and an extended sabbatical that, for me, have been a source of enormous good in giving myself a break. Then you can assess the measure of your own soul and adapt these to fit you.

Consider a Recurring Sabbatical

God is the one who established a created order around recurring rhythms, from the daily rotation of the earth to our annual circuit around the sun and every rhythm in between. This pervasive reality begs us to establish our own rhythms of soul care. While there is no one-size-fits-all, consider an approach to rest and Sabbath that looks like this:

- One hour a day
- One day a week
- One (extra) day a month
- One weekend a quarter
- One week a year

Don't get confused. This is not vacation; this is soul-cation. What does one do for soul care in times of Sabbath or sabbatical? Here is my recipe: refresh, reflect, and refocus. In that order.

1. Refresh

For me, to refresh is to detox. I sit outside in a quiet, beautiful space and commune with nature. I turn off my mind. Shed the layers of worry and pressure. Breathe in the sunshine. Feel the textures of light, temperature, and sound. Don't pray except for the spontaneous exclamations of joy. Or sorrow, for that matter. This is primal, and it's an IV into your soul.

2. Reflect

Once the refresh process has run its course and you're beginning to feel human again (as in emotionally grounded, physically renewed, spiritually awakened), then it's time to reflect. This is the time to look back. How far back? However far is helpful. Ask yourself this: What are the trends? What is the message of your life from past weeks? What is God's heart for you in this moment? This is a great time to journal as you absorb the learning of this season in preparation for recalibration.

274

3. Refocus

Now, and only now, is it time to look ahead. Where is your current trajectory headed? Is that the right destination? What mid-course corrections are being called for in your journey? This is where you can engage the strategic process to realign and define what's most important for you in this next season: spiritually, relationally, vocationally, financially, and so forth.

The beauty of this simple process is that it is eminently scalable. Easily adapted to a thirty-minute daily practice or a week's personal retreat, which I personally like to take somewhere between Christmas and mid-January to renew my vision for the coming year.

Consider an Extended Sabbatical

At this point, allow me to passionately pitch the idea of extended sabbaticals. While weekly rhythms of Sabbath are expected in the Christian community, the practice of taking several weeks (or even months) for this purpose is rare indeed. Yet an extended sabbatical is an established spiritual practice dating back millennia, one that is tailor-made for our current culture of "muchness and manyness," as the esteemed Richard Foster aptly names it. "In contemporary society our adversary majors in three things: noise, hurry, and crowds. If he can keep us engaged in 'muchness' and 'manyness,' he will rest satisfied."

If this message resonates with you, give yourself a break. Your soul will be glad you did. Actually, everyone you know will be glad, including your clients.

Coaching the Coach Tip

Pull out your calendar right now. Within the next thirty days, block off one entire day to give yourself a break. (You can do more than a day, but I urge you not to do less.) Now decide where to spend it—somewhere intrinsically refreshing and completely buffered from interruption and technology. Come on, unplug. Next, share this commitment with a trusted ally who will hold you to it. Then do it. Let me know how it goes!

About Our Contributing Coaches

Kim Avery is founder and president of Kim Avery Coaching, a coaching and mentoring firm that helps Christian coaches market successfully and coach masterfully. She is a licensed mental health counselor, professional certified coach, board certified coach, and trains coaches at the Professional Christian Coaching Institute and The Academies. Kim's mission is to help others live Christ-saturated, joy-filled, and purpose-driven lives. You can pick up a copy of her free e-book *Top Ten Marketing Mistakes NOT to Make* at www. KimAveryCoaching.com.

Dwight Bain is a pioneer Christian coach and executive director of the International Christian Coaching Association. He has dedicated his life to guiding people toward greater results. He is an author, a nationally certified counselor, and certified life coach, in practice since 1984. He has spoken to more than 3,000 groups including Disney, Toyota, and AT&T. As a trusted media resource, he has been interviewed and quoted in newspapers/websites including *The New York Times, Chicago Tribune, Atlanta Journal*, FoxBusiness.com, and MSNBC.com. www.DwightBain.com.

Denise Baumann has been married for more than thirty years and has four children including one with special needs. Denise has been a life coach for more than three years and is a member of AACC and ICCA. "Jeremiah 29:11 tells us God has a plan for our lives, and I love helping my clients discover and add clarity to the plan God has for them." To contact Denise, email her at lifecoach@denisebaumann.com or check out her website at www.denisebaumann.com.

Dr. Katie Brazelton, Ph.D., M.Div., M.A., is an ICCA board member and Rockbridge Seminary board member. She is founder of Life Purpose Coaching Centers International®, a coach-training provider approved by ICF, CCE-BCC, and IACET to offer continuing education units. Katie is a sought-after coach, 2-Day LifePlan facilitator, and speaker worldwide, as well as a bestselling author with eight books and three DVD coaching curricula about life purpose. www.LifePurposeCoachingCenters.com.

Dr. Tim Clinton, Ed.D., is president of the nearly 50,000-member American Association of Christian Counselors, the largest and most diverse Christian counseling association in the world. He is the professor of counseling and pastoral care and executive director of the Center for Counseling and Family Studies at Liberty University. Tim now spends a majority of his time working with Christian leaders and professional athletes. He is recognized as a world leader in faith and mental health issues and has authored seventeen books including his latest, *God Attachment*.

Dr. Henry Cloud, Ph.D., is a coach, leadership consultant, clinical psychologist, and author of several best-selling books including *Necessary Endings: The Employees, Businesses, and Relationships That All of Us Have To Give Up In Order to Move Forward*. His most recent book is *Boundaries for Leaders: Results, Relationships, and being Ridiculously in Charge*. For more information and resources, visit www.drcloud.com.

Vicki Corrington is a professional certified coach, certified professional Christian coach, certified Myers-Briggs practitioner, and board certified coach. She is an experienced life, mentor, and retreat coach who uses professional tools such as Myers-Briggs assessments to enhance individual, couples, and group coaching. Vicki serves on the faculty of Professional Christian Coaching

Institute, a distinctly Christian coach training school, and is a member of the International Coach Federation, International Christian Coaching Association, and Christian Coaches Network. Visit www.coachvicki.com to learn more.

Dr. Mark Crear, Ph.D. is not only an anointed man of God but also the president of Mark Crear Ministries, an ordained pastor, published author, board certified professional Christian counselor, certified life and business coach, and an Olympic champion. Mark is a board member of the International Christian Coaches Association, the director of counseling for The Family Church International, and director of BAACC, the culturally competent division of the American Association of Christian Counselors. www.markcrearministries.com.

Diane Cunningham is the founder and president of the National Association of Christian Women Entrepreneurs. She is a "business therapist," plane-crash survivor, author, consultant, speaker, marathon runner, and fun friend. Find out more about NACWE and why 165 women joined in the first year at www.NACWE.org. Connect with Diane at www.facebook.com/DianeCunningham for fun updates, silly videos, and lively conversation.

Elizabeth Gaston Cunningham is an accredited business communicator and credentialed Christian life coach with 35 years of experience leading corporate communications and public relations in for-profit and nonprofit organizations. Formerly executive director of employee communications and ethics at financial services giant USAA, Elizabeth now serves as special assistant at Hope for the Heart, a worldwide biblical counseling ministry, where she assists with social media, trade books, public relations, and a variety of other communication projects.

Jerome Daley is on a mission to help leaders thrive. Thrive in their inner lives, thrive in their outer leadership. The author of seven books and former publisher of *Christian Coaching Magazine*, Jerome is a leadership coach, business consultant, trainer, and speaker. He is married to Kellie and loves having three teenagers; they make their home in Greensboro, North Carolina, where Jerome enjoys hiking, cycling, rock climbing, and most anything that takes him outside. Learn more at www.iThrive9.com.

Dr. Jennifer Degler is a licensed psychologist, life coach, and co-author of *No More Christian Nice Girl: When Just Being Nice—Instead of Good—Hurts You, Your Family, and Your Friends*. Her coaching specialties include small business development, career transitions, coaching the coach, and making a good marriage a great marriage. She leads marriage and women's retreats across the country and is the founder of CWIVES, an organization devoted to helping Christian wives enhance their sexuality (www.cwives.com). Visit her website at www.jenniferdegler.com.

Anne Denmark, is a professional certified coach with the International Coach Federation. She serves on the faculty of Professional Christian Coaching Institute, the largest distinctly Christian coach training school aligned with the standards of ICF. Connect with Anne at Anne@lifediscoverycoaching.com and visit her website at www.ProfessionalChristianCoaching.com.

Dr. Evelyn de Villiers is a licensed clinical psychologist and a member of the American Psychological Association, the International Christian Coaching Association, and an alumni member of Dr. John Townsend's Life Coaching Program. She teaches and speaks at churches, schools, conferences, and retreats. Her office is in La Jolla,

California, and she lives with her husband in San Diego where they are empty nesters after raising their blended family of seven children. They have a very handsome grandson whom they love to spoil.

Jennifer Cisney Ellers is a professional counselor, life coach, crisis response trainer, author, and speaker. She does training, counseling, and coaching in the field of grief, crisis, and trauma through the Institute for Compassionate Care. Jennifer also does divorce coaching, training, and speaking through Emerge Victorious, a ministry for women rebuilding their lives after divorce. She is the co-author of *The First 48 Hours: Spiritual Caregivers as First Responders.* She also co-authored *Emerge Victorious: A Woman's Transformational Guide After Her Divorce.*

Shannon Ethridge, M.A., is an AACC-certified life coach, an internationally sought-after conference speaker, and the best-selling author of nineteen books on healthy sexuality and spirituality. She also mentors aspiring writers and speakers through her online mentorship program B.L.A.S.T. (Building Leaders, Authors, Speakers, and Teachers). Her greatest passion, however, is being a wife to husband Greg and a mom and cheerleader to their two adult children, Erin and Matthew. Learn more about Shannon Ethridge Ministries or B.L.A.S.T. at www.shannonethridge.com or www.blastmentoring. com.

Rosemary Flaaten, M.A., B.Ed., is a life coach, spiritual director, author, speaker, workshop presenter, and adjunct professor at Rocky Mountain College. She specializes in personal development and relationship coaching, as well as career, transition, and leadership coaching. Rosemary is widely published, including her best-selling book *A Woman and Her Relationships* and *A Woman and Her Workplace.*

Her breadth of experience and education makes her an internationally sought-after speaker by secular and Christian organizations, including the American Association of Christian Counselors.

Dr. Sylvia Hart Frejd is a counselor, certified life coach, and director of training for Flourish in Life and Relationships Coaching offering life coaching and coach training. She is a speaker and worship leader for conferences and retreats worldwide and a published songwriter with Integrity Music. Sylvia has presented at the AACC World, National, and Marriage conferences and is featured on the Life Coach training DVDs. Her new book *The Digital Invasion* is coming in June 2013. www.TheDigitalInvasion.com.

Linda Gilden is an author, speaker, editor, and writing coach. As director of writing programs for CLASSEMINARS, Inc., the CLASS Christian Writers Conference, and the Carolina Christian Writers Conference, Linda encourages others to clearly communicate God's love to the world. With more than a thousand published articles and several books, she specializes in coaching writers to communicate with excellence as they achieve their publication dreams. Linda is a member of the International Christian Coaches Association. For more information, visit www.LindaGilden.com.

Linda Goldfarb is a board certified professional coach with ICCA, a certified advanced personalities coach with CLASSEMINARS, Inc., a fitness specialist with the Cooper Institute, and a professional actress. She specializes in relational transformation and presentation coaching. Linda is passionate about helping families and individuals communicate more effectively to empower their communities. Her strengths include wellness management, personality dynamics, and relational growth. For more information, visit www.lindagoldfarb.com.

Martha Greene is a speaker, author, and certified professional life coach. She specializes in spiritual formation coaching, partnering with her clients to enable them to live fully alive in their relationship with God, others, and themselves. Her passion is helping men and women walk intimately with God and live in His unique calling on their lives—in every role and with every assignment they have been given. Martha can be reached at martha@coachingfullyalive.com.

June Hunt founded the biblical counseling ministry of Hope For The Heart in 1986. Today it offers biblical hope and practical help in twenty-seven languages and more than sixty countries. June's Biblical Counseling Library provides in-depth insights into 100 topics. Her teaching is featured in monthly Biblical Counseling Institutes and on two daily radio programs: *Hope For The Heart* and *Hope In The Night*, dedicated to presenting God's truth for today's problems. Connect with June on her Facebook at June.Hunt.Hope or at www. HopeForTheHeart.org.

Linda Beck Johnson is a professional life coach, consultant, trainer, change management facilitator, and leadership advisor. Her coaching specialties include leading change, the people side of effective transformation, and working with women in life planning. After thirty-five years in the corporate world, working for financial services giant USAA, Linda now teaches and facilitates workshops and retreats.

Linda Knasel, M.A., LPC, is a nationally board certified coach and counselor. She lives in the midwest and is married with two children. Linda is CEO of Walking Towards Solutions and G.R.O.W., and an independent contractor for Desert Streams Christian Counseling.

Linda has taught at several colleges and universities including Cornerstone University, Western Michigan University, University of Phoenix, and Kalamazoo Valley Community College. She is an active member of the American Christian Counseling Association and International Christian Coaching Association.

Sandra Dopf Lee is a divorce coach, mediator, speaker, and author. Sandra is the founder of Emerge Victorious, LLC and co-author and producer of *The Next Steps* DVD video curriculum for women transforming their lives after divorce. She equips other coaches through her Divorce Coach Training program. Divorce changes life stories and God still has a life plan for them, but they often need a coach to help guide them through and beyond this process. www.EmergeVictorious.com. 800-615-6708.

Dr. Dave Martin is known by many around the world as America's No. 1 Christian success coach, and he speaks regularly at churches, colleges, corporations, and conferences. He is the author of several best-selling books including *The 12 Traits of the Greats* and *The Force of Favor*. Dr. Dave is founder and president of Dave Martin International, which exists to serve the local church, business organizations, leaders, and individuals. Along with several other board positions, Dr. Dave currently sits on the advisory board of Joel Osteen's Champions Network, and he works hard to give back, to be a blessing, and to sow into the lives of others.

Kevin W. McCarthy is the chief leadership officer at On-Purpose Partners in Winter Park, Florida. He is the author of the groundbreaking book series *The On-Purpose Person* and *The On-Purpose Business Person*. The four major obstacles to change and how to overcome them are addressed in his book *FIT 4 Leading: Discover the Joy From Taking a Hard Look at Yourself*. To learn more, go to www.onpurpose.com and www.FIT4Leading.com.

Christopher McCluskey, M.S.W., PCC, is president and CEO of Professional Christian Coaching Institute, a distance-learning school aligned with the standards of the International Coach Federation. His highly acclaimed teleclass *The Accidental Entrepreneur* and weekly podcasts titled *Professional Christian Coaching—Live!* have enabled thousands of coaches throughout the world to establish successful practices. Called by many the "Father of Christian Coaching," Chris has shaped this emerging field through his frequent teaching, writing, keynoting, and service on numerous boards. www. ProfessionalChristianCoaching.com.

Dr. Linda Mintle, Ph.D., coaches clients in the areas of relationships, life balance, and food and weight issues. She is a best-selling author with eighteen titles. Dr. Mintle is a licensed therapist, professor, national speaker, paid blogger for BeliefNet, and a media expert. With thirty years of experience working with people in all types of settings, coaching has been a rewarding way for Linda to help people maximize their strengths, set goals, and take positive steps toward their life goals.

Lisa Gomez Osborn is the president and founder of Paragraphs 22 Coaching & Consulting. Lisa has worked with others for more than fifteen years in areas such as overcoming personal and spiritual growth obstacles, leadership development, organizational development, Christian life coach training, personality profiling, communication, and conflict resolution. Lisa is passionate about Christian coaching and helping other coaches build their businesses. LifeCoachLisaOsborn.com or lisa@LifeCoachLisaOsborn.com.

Renee Oscarson is a certified life coach through the Institute for Life Coach Training and a board certified coach (Center for Credentialing and Education). She completed additional coaching coursework at the Professional Christian Coaching Institute and Potentials Realized. As a university professor and life coach, she specializes in human development and aging, assisting individuals and organizations navigating caregiving, midlife issues, and preparation for retirement. She is passionate about using coaching as a vehicle for racial and cultural reconciliation among communities and groups.

Michael Pfau, M.Ed., PCC, BCC, is founder and president of Crossways Life Coaching, LLC, a coaching, mentoring, and training business. Michael partners with financial planners to guide their baby boomer clients to create a life of purpose, passion, and significance. Along with his own successful coaching practice, Michael has logged hundreds of hours as an instructor for the Professional Christian Coaching Institute and also serves as an adjunct professor for the Assemblies of God Theological Seminary. More about Michael at www.CrosswaysLifeCoaching.com.

Karen Porter is an international speaker, author, and coach. She helps aspiring writers and speakers develop messages and careers. She is owner of *k*ae Creative Solutions, a communications coaching firm. She and her husband, George, own Bold Vision Books, a full-service traditional publishing house. They live near Houston, Texas, with their peaceful Great Pyrenees, Isabelle. Find more information about Karen and Bold Vision Books at www.karenporter.com and www.boldvisionbooks.com.

Matthew Reed is a coach, speaker, and blogger. Before entering coaching, Matthew spent sixteen years pastoring at two dynamic and fast-growing churches. His specialty is helping professionals, particularly those in medicine, who are successful in the workplace achieve the same level of success in their personal lives. In addition to coaching, he serves on the steering team of Christ Healthcare

Ministry of Orange/Sullivan Co. NY, a free clinic seeking to share the Gospel through medicine. For more information about Matthew, visit www.matthewreedcoaching.com.

Dr. John Rottschafer is a certified life and relationship coach with a lengthy history as a clinical psychologist. His passion for healthy relationships comes from the belief that relationships are one of the most powerful forces on earth. John coaches individuals, couples, and families, along with corporate management teams. Through writing and speaking, he promotes the message of personal, relational, and spiritual growth. John is also an adjunct professor of psychology at Kuyper College in Grand Rapids, Michigan.

Dr. Eric Scalise, Ph.D., is the vice president for professional development with the American Association of Christian Counselors, the former chair of counseling programs at Regent University and the president of LIV Enterprises & Consulting. He is a licensed professional counselor and a licensed marriage and family therapist with more than thirty-two years of clinical and professional experience in the mental health field. He is an author, a national and international conference speaker, and frequently consults with organizations, clinicians, ministry leaders, and churches on a variety of issues.

Cheryl Scanlan, PCC, CPCC, is a former executive with a multi-million-dollar firm. Cheryl combines strong business acumen with a passion for the Christian coaching industry to facilitate the development of confident ambassadors for Christ in both corporate and ministry environments. She mentors coaches across the country and coaches pastoral and director teams to strengthen the core of church bodies. For more information on Cheryl Scanlan, visit wayoflifecoaching.com.

Diane Schroeder is a life coach who is building her practice while pursuing her education. She is a student in the psychology program at Cornerstone University in Grand Rapids, Michigan, and entering Grand Rapids Theological Seminary in the fall of 2013 to obtain her master's degree in counseling. Diane has been married to her best friend, Dan, for more than twenty years and is the proud mom of teenagers Kelly and Samuel and her misfit canine Dusty Dog.

Georgia Shaffer, M.A., is a professional speaker, certified life coach and the author of four books including *Coaching the Coach: Life Coaching Stories and Tips for Transforming Lives.* She is a regular columnist for *Christian Coaching Today* and a board member of the International Christian Coaches Association. Georgia is on the teaching team of AACC's Professional Life Coaching Training. She specializes in coaching coaches, women, and communicators. To find out more, visit www.GeorgiaShaffer.com.

Mary Sorrentino is a certified professional life coach, technical coach and trainer, author, speaker, and founder of Joy on Purpose Life Coaching, LLC and CoachTech Services. As a professional life coach, Mary's mission is to support those who support others. Mary serves on the faculty of Professional Christian Coaching Institute, where she teaches technology for coaches. With more than two decades in corporate information technology, Mary now provides computer coaching and training through CoachTech Services. Visit Mary online at www.CoachTechServices.com and www.JoyOnPurpose.com.

Dr. David Stoop, Ph.D., is a licensed clinical psychologist in California. He is the founder and director of The Center for Family Therapy in Newport Beach, California, where he has his counseling practice. He is an adjunct professor at Fuller Seminary and serves on the executive board of the American Association of Christian

Counselors. Dr. Stoop is often heard as the co-host of the national *New Life* radio program. He and his wife, Jan, live in Newport Beach and have three sons and six grandchildren.

Pam Taylor is passionately in love with Jesus Christ and delights in walking intimately with Him and helping other women do the same. Pam lived as a missionary to third world countries and was a single homeschooling mom to her two (now grown) children. Pam received her training at the Professional Christian Coaching Institute, but she's proudest of her unofficial coach training from the school of life's experiences. Find out more about Pam's work with coaches and moms at www.LoavesandFishesCoaching.com.

Dr. John Townsend is a leadership coach, organizational consultant, psychologist, and author. He teaches and trains on success and growth principles. John has sold more than six million copies of his books and is heard by three million listeners on *New Life* radio. He conducts his own leadership coaching programs in Newport Beach, California; Dallas, Texas; and Indianapolis, Indiana. drtownsend.com.

Leslie Vernick is a popular speaker, author, licensed clinical social worker, and relationship coach with a private counseling practice in Pennsylvania. She is the author of seven books, including the best-selling *The Emotionally Destructive Relationship*. Leslie has had the privilege to teach in Iraq, Russia, Romania, Hungary, and the Philippines, and is featured in three of the American Association of Christian Counselor video teaching series videos. For more information, visit Leslie's website at www.leslievernick.com.

Dr. Catherine Hart Weber is a licensed therapist, specializing in Flourish In Life and Relationships coaching and training, intensives, growth groups, and retreats. She has been a frequent and key instructor at several universities as well as on the American Association of Christian Counselor's Professional Coaching DVD series. She serves on the AACC advisory board of directors. Explore the Flourish blog and relevant resources for coaching at her website www.howtoflourish.com.

Susan Whitcomb is a leading authority and media resource on career and leadership coach certification training, and the author of eight books featured in retailer booksellers worldwide, including *The Christian's Career Journey, Resumè Magic,* and *30-Day Job Promotion* (JIST Publishing). An inspirational presenter and engaging trainer, Susan has logged more than 3,000 hours teaching the Certified Career Management Coach program, Certified Executive & Leadership Development Coach program, Certified Job Search Strategist program, and Certified Social Media Career Strategist program offered through www.TheAcademies.com.

Nancy Williams, M.Ed., LPC is a licensed professional counselor, life coach, trainer, speaker, and author of *Secrets to Parenting Your Adult Child* (Bethany House, 2011). Her coaching specialties include supporting women who are moving through life transitions and entering new life stages, women in business, and working with family relationship challenges.

Kathy Carlton Willis owns KCW Communications, specializing in publicity and marketing. She coaches writers to achieve their goals. Kathy is also a pastor's wife and inspires women to have "aha" light bulb moments through Scripture application. She's a member of

Advanced Writers and Speakers Association and serves on faculty with Christian Leaders Authors and Speaker seminars. She writes and speaks on the issues that hold women back, and she shines the light on their path to freedom.

Mary Yerkes is a Christian coach, professional writer, seasoned mentor, and spiritual companion who values intimacy with Jesus Christ and reflective living in God's presence. She helps people live and lead from the inside out. Mary's training is through the Professional Christian Coaching Institute. She holds memberships in several professional organizations, including the Christian Coaches Network, the International Coach Federation, the International Christian Coaching Association, the National Association of Independent Writers and Editors, and the International Association of Business Communicators. Visit www.newlifechristiancoaching.com and www.maryyerkes.com to learn more.

About Georgia Shaffer

Georgia is a regular columnist in Christian Coaching Today and a board member of the International Christian Coaching Association. She was the first woman coach trained by John Maxwell's Leadership Program in 2002. She is also an instructor with the American Association of Christian Counselor's Professional Coaching DVD series. With more than eleven years of coaching experience, Georgia specializes in the following:

- Coaching the coach
- Coaching for authors and speakers
- Life coaching for women
- Relationship coaching for singles

In addition to being a certified life coach, Georgia is a professional speaker and a licensed psychologist in Pennsylvania. Georgia speaks frequently at professional conferences, women's retreats, and singles and cancer survivor events helping people identify answers to the questions "What needs to grow? What needs to go?" in their life.

Georgia is also the author of *Taking Out Your Emotional Trash, How NOT to Date a Loser,* and *A Gift of Mourning Glories,* all of which can be found at www.GeorgiaShaffer.com. Her new book *Avoiding the 12 Relationship Mistakes Women Make* will be released in January 2014.

The film *Letters to God* features Georgia's story of how in 1991, after a recurrence of breast cancer, Georgia was given a two percent chance to live an additional ten years. "At that time my son Kyle was only eight years old," she said, "which meant I had almost no chance to see him graduate from high school. Not only did I see Kyle graduate from high school and then college, but when Kyle was thirty, I had the joy of dancing with him at his wedding."

Georgia has also appeared on television shows such as *The 700 Club, The Sharron and Hermann Show, Decision Today, Sky Angel's A Time for Hope*, and on the DVD *Jesus: Fact or Fiction?*

When she isn't writing, speaking, or coaching, Georgia enjoys spending time with her son's family and also deciding what needs to grow or go in her scenic garden. She resides near Lancaster, Pennsylvania.

What Georgia's coaching clients are saying about working with her:

"Georgia Shaffer is an extraordinary person and a powerfully effective coach. Her integrity inspires me, and her persistent belief in my capabilities fosters within me a spirit of accomplishment that has been absolutely priceless."

---Lisa Gomez Osborn, president, Paragraphs 22
Coaching and Consulting

"Georgia Shaffer was a tremendous blessing to me in helping me craft my keynote speeches. She is kind, articulate, and insightful. I would recommend her."

---Anne Beiler, founder, Auntie Anne's Pretzels,
Gap, Pennsylvania

"My life coaching experience was so much more wonderful and beneficial than I anticipated. Georgia certainly has a divine craft, with her skillful ability to identify barriers and a true grit for asking the difficult questions."

---Anna Flores, Peace Corp Volunteer in the Philippines